GOD
INSPIRED

God Inspired:

A Life Worth Living

Benjamin R. Dever

PALMETTO
PUBLISHING
Charleston, SC
www.PalmettoPublishing.com

Copyright © 2023 by Benjamin R. Dever

All rights reserved.

No portion of this book may be reproduced, stored in a retrieval system, or transmitted in any form by any means–electronic, mechanical, photocopy, recording, or other–except for brief quotations in printed reviews, without prior permission of the author.

Paperback ISBN: 979-8-8229-0912-0
eBook ISBN: 979-8-8229-0913-7

*I dedicate this book to Fiona,
my beautiful daughter,
whom I love dearly.*

Table of Contents

Chapter 1	Childhood	1
Chapter 2	Saved	3
Chapter 3	Child of God	6
Chapter 4	I Am a Seeker	9
Chapter 5	Searching	11
Chapter 6	Forgive and Remember	14
Chapter 7	Loving My Enemies	19
Chapter 8	Live My Best Life	22
Chapter 9	Gentle Jesus	24
Chapter 10	Fall in Love with Jesus	27
Chapter 11	Trust	30
Chapter 12	Be Humble	34
Chapter 13	Moral Compass	38
Chapter 14	Beautiful World	46
Chapter 15	Be Obsessed with Jesus	50
Chapter 16	Meant for Eternity	53
Chapter 17	Jesus Won Me Over	56
Chapter 18	Peace	59

Chapter 19	Metaphor	64
Chapter 20	A Still, Small Voice	67
Chapter 21	Intimacy	70
Chapter 22	The Good News	80
Chapter 23	Sanctification	84
Chapter 24	Beyond a Reasonable Doubt	87
Chapter 25	Safety	91
Chapter 26	Finding a New Life	95
Chapter 27	Work Is a Gift from God	99
Chapter 28	Strength in Humility	102
Chapter 29	Free Will	108
Chapter 30	Don't Worry	111
Chapter 31	Empathy	115
Chapter 32	Familiar Words	119
Chapter 33	Knowing Is Half the Battle	122
Chapter 34	The Armor of God	125
Chapter 35	Belt of Truth	127
Chapter 36	Breastplate of Righteousness	129
Chapter 37	Shoes of Peace	131
Chapter 38	Shield of Faith	134
Chapter 39	Helmet of Salvation	136
Chapter 40	Sword of the Spirit	139
Chapter 41	Pray at All Times	142
Chapter 42	Human Rights	147
Chapter 43	I Have Peace	150

CHAPTER 1
Childhood

I guess one could say that I had a less than ideal childhood—my mother wasn't around much and my father seemed to think that I was everything that was wrong with his life; most of the time, I was left to myself.

In the beginning, my father would come find me and pour his miseries and fears out into me. I believe he was using me as his personal wastebasket to unload all of his insecurities into. Dad would tell me how disappointed he was in me and follow that up with violent beatings. My dad seemed to make sure that I understood that I was the reason his life was so terrible.

I was devastated to learn that I was a defective product—I was more like a disease or a curse; doomed to a life of failure because I am the definition of failure, according to my dad. My father was terrifying and my mother wasn't around. I felt terrible about myself, and I wanted to do everything I could to make it easier on the people around me. I worked hard on damage control; I tried to make people laugh because my life needed to be one giant apology for being born.

When my mother was there...she would take a moment to tell me about magical faeries that lived across the road in a giant faerie tree. I would look out the window, absolutely amazed by this. I would turn to ask my mom more about the faerie tree, and I would see the last of her disappearing out the front door of the house—she was gone.

In the beginning, when I hurt myself, I would inadvertently run to my mom. She would look down at me with a giant strange smile and ask me if I was crying. Of course I was crying. She would ask me if Conan would cry; she knew that I liked *Conan the Barbarian* comic books. She would admonish me for crying by reminding me that Conan wouldn't cry. I would feel ashamed and force myself to stop crying.

I always had the feeling that I was burdening my mother, so I would try hard not to bother her. It was pointless to run to my mother. Mom made it clear that I wasn't to turn to her for help. She didn't want to bother with me because of what Dad said about me. I figured that I was quite the burden for my mother because I was hopelessly defective and subhuman.

I had four siblings—two brothers and two sisters. Our parents would get into violent confrontations often. We would cling together in a room, scared out of our minds. We would huddle together and listen to my mom scream and my dad punching her. Sometimes something would smash. I thought my dad was killing my mom; this happened countless times. I felt that we were close as children but I think, rather, we had a common bond in terror. We suffered together. We had a bond, but it was a bond made of fear. I am sad as I think about it—we didn't stand a chance.

My world was chaos and my master was fear. I had no reason to hope or believe that there was anything good. I was born into a world much like a prison camp. I was set adrift in an ocean of chaos with no land in sight. But then something happened...

CHAPTER 2

SAVED

I had been to church many times before; my father insisted that we go to church every Sunday. Sundays were the worst with my father—he would be especially mean on Sundays. Church was a tradition in my family. My father's obsession with going to church rivaled his ability to be cruel; they seemed inextricably intertwined with each other. Like a horror movie, my father would talk about Jesus from time to time then abuse me violently and ruthlessly.

One Sunday was different, however—very different. My dad decided to visit another church one Sunday, I don't know why. I think I had just started elementary school at the time. I am not sure of my age because I tried to forget those years.

I remember getting drawn in by what the speaker was saying that day. I had never heard anything like it. The speaker wasn't the usual preacher for that church—I found out many years later that he was a preacher that moved around. He was only visiting that Sunday because he was a traveling preacher.

The preacher was talking about Jesus Christ. He explained that Jesus came to die for my sins and the sins of the world. He explained that humanity is broken by sin and they need to reconnect with God to fix that brokenness; when he mentioned that man is depraved and broken in need of a Savior...he had my attention.

I lived in a dark world of bondage and slavery. I was hopelessly overwhelmed and helpless to do anything about it. I was a small child in a world where I was powerless. I could see that I couldn't save myself—I needed God to rescue me.

I was told that Jesus was perfect and without sin, and the world killed him for this. I believed that he was killed for being good because I lived in such a dark world. I was told by the speaker that love is the answer to our problems. If people started loving each other, then the world would be a better place.

I loved Jesus and how he was wanting to help me. I immediately submitted to Jesus and accepted him as my Lord and Savior. I felt a tremendous peace and love in that moment. It was, as if, in the middle of a long cold winter the sun came out for a moment and warmed the air. I fell in love with Jesus that day.

My dad sat with me through the exact same message as I heard. How did my dad not hear the message of love? I tried to tell my dad about Jesus but he didn't want to hear about it. I was devastated. I told my dad that we only have to love each other and we can be happy. I said this in the parking lot after church that day. My dad told me to get in the car through clenched teeth. I was perplexed—I didn't know why my dad couldn't see what I did. That was the day I was saved.

I was excited about Jesus but no one else around me felt the same. The joy I felt from that day lasted a couple weeks. Eventually it got drowned out by more beatings and the misery of the world; eventually I questioned whether it was even real. I lost touch with that day—although what stuck with me was a sense that I was valuable. I felt a sense of outrage about how I was being treated welling up within me.

A fire was lit that day in my belly. A fire that said I was a human being; that I was worthy. Jesus said I am his now. I became a child of the king that day—the King of Kings. I started finding the courage to stand up for myself. I started fighting for myself after I was saved. I didn't realize, until many years later, that it was Jesus in my heart giving me the desire to fight for myself.

Later, I realized, the day I first believed in Jesus made me the single most dangerous person on the planet against evil. As angry as I was against God for allowing these horrible things to happen to me...I had a much deeper hatred for evil. As I challenged God's character and remained honest with myself, I could see that evil was my enemy, not God. Each time I brought my questions to God, I could see that it wasn't God who was hurting me—the world had tortured and killed God...I felt comfort in knowing that Jesus suffered as I had.

I was an innocent child that was violently abused and neglected. I did nothing wrong. Jesus didn't do anything wrong, either. As an abused child, I felt an advocate in Jesus Christ. Jesus knew exactly what it's like to be both completely innocent and horribly victimized. Jesus gets me.

I had no problem admitting my sins and asking for forgiveness—I could see clearly that I was helpless and surrounded by depravity. A terrible evil is in the world and I had an extreme prejudice against evil. I came to this understanding after I met Jesus. I decided that I will never allow anyone to control me again. I declared to myself: "Never again!"

CHAPTER 3

Child of God

At the time, I was fuzzy about what the problem could be with my life. I understood that I didn't like the way I was being treated, but I couldn't see how damaging the abuse was. In hindsight, I can see that the God of the universe personally received me into his care. God's word, the Bible, in John 10:28 says: "I give them eternal life, and they will never perish; no one will snatch them out of my hand."

God's word also told me in John 1:12: "Yet to all who did receive him, to those who believed in his name, he gave the right to become children of God." At the time, I was my parents' child and beholden to all the nature thereof—my parents were all I knew. As far as I was concerned, I was completely at the mercy of my parents and their limitations. In my mind, there was no escaping what nature had produced in me.

I was a slave to the constructs of mortal man. What's done is done. My parents were God to my child mind; they had all power and control over me. My parents were God in my small vulnerable mind. Why should I think otherwise? My parents exercised complete dominion over me.

My father told me I was worthless and used violence to make sure I understood this truth. My mother wanted nothing to do with me, which reinforced the realization that what my father said was true. I was hopelessly condemned to a life of failure and emptiness—it was fate.

At the same time, Jesus gave me "the right to become children of God." (John 1:12) After I accepted Jesus and believed in him, I had introduced a contradicting narrative into my mind; I had become a child of God. The competing narrative against being doomed to a life of slavery had been planted in my soul. I found a small foothold to begin to learn who Jesus is and if he is actually true.

A child of God?! Imagine the implications of being a child of God. Here is an attempt to understand the implications. What would my life look like if my father was a king? I would have all the privileges that come with that; I would be living as royalty. I would be from a special bloodline. I would feel entitled to be treated with honor and respect. If someone treated me bad, I would recognize it, right away, and confront that person.

I would feel that I truly mattered if I believed I was special. I would believe that I have the power to make change in the world. I would believe in myself to accomplish almost anything I set my mind to. I would be receiving a huge inheritance. I would be a man of prominence, value, and importance.

All of these beliefs run in direct contradiction to the world I was born into. Jesus made me a child of God, which includes all the privileges that come with that. I had been bought at a price to become a prince and receive all of the privileges therein.

These new beliefs started a war in me for my very soul. A conflict erupted that I couldn't avoid. My heart raged over the idea that I could be valuable; a precedent had been set by Jesus claiming me as his own. Everything that I was conditioned to believe went to war against the notion that I was now of royal blood. I had to face the idea that life is meaningful, that there is a purpose to everything, and that evil will be held accountable.

A spark was lit in my soul that was burning with a holy fire—no evil thought could sit comfortably in my mind without it coming under the scrutiny of this terrible goodness; a goodness so pure that it demanded every bit of my strength to seize it. Any sort of tyranny does not withstand the onslaught of the pure love that I had surrendered to—this loving, holy fire threatened to consume everything I understood about the world up to that point. I was terrified of this new force and yet also completely enchanted with the possibility that I could dare to believe I am so special.

Whole nations have gone to war over the concept of a human being having infinite value. I had entered into a lineage of women and men who could not tolerate any form of evil—I had become a believer.

CHAPTER 4

I Am a Seeker

These revelations about being valuable slowly took hold of me. For many years I had forgotten about accepting Jesus Christ as my savior because I was so young; I didn't fully understand that I had entered a relationship with Jesus Christ.

Like any relationship, one must invest in it if you want meaning from that relationship. I had learned about who Jesus was from the people I grew up around. I heard pastors, my grandmother, movies, my dad, my siblings, even my friends...all had an opinion about who Jesus is. I was not impressed with what they would say. The day I accepted Jesus as my Lord and Savior eventually came to be overwhelmed with the cares of this world; the experience lost its power and meaning in my life over time.

I began to pursue my dreams. I saw Jesus as a nice idea, but he wasn't relevant to everyday living. Jesus was a nice story but was not practical for living.

The feelings of despair, helplessness, and hopelessness were still nagging me through everything I did. I had pursued some lofty goals, and when those didn't pan out, I started seeking God for answers. I had no idea whether there was a God or not; I believed that it probably couldn't be known. I decided to try to find out for myself if God was real—I was feeling hopeless and stuck at the time.

I was always looking for purpose in some form or another. I was reading philosophy books and studying about meaning and purpose. In the beginning I was not searching in Christianity for answers; I came from a family who considered themselves Christians, yet seemed about as lost as I was at the time. I was looking in both secular and Christan sources.

Eventually, I decided to fully commit to finding answers in Christianity. Christian authors kept drawing me in because of their description of the human condition. I was drawn to the writers that remained intellectually honest and were humble in nature.

The secular authors would talk about "finding themselves" or reaching a place of "enlightenment." I didn't believe that these people found enlightenment—I felt that they were blind to their own human condition. I was convinced that human beings are mostly self-centered, narcissistic, and unreliable. I wasn't going to trust anyone that claimed they had meaning and purpose figured out on their own.

Reading Ecclesiastes is what helped me to explore Christianity. Ecclesiastes is a book of the Christian Bible. The book talked about how the world is meaningless and without purpose. I understood that to be true, and so it was a good starting point for me. The author of Ecclesiastes seemed to be in a place where I was. He was despairing about how meaningless the world is. I decided to pursue Christianity because I believed this author was telling the truth. I appreciated the author being honest, yet he was also a believer?! How strange and intriguing—I was hooked.

CHAPTER 5

Searching

I didn't understand that I was building a relationship with God until years later. Building a relationship takes time, and good relationships stand the test of time. My relationship with Jesus was immature in the beginning, but as the years went on my relationship matured.

When I first thought of Jesus, I saw him as weak. There was a picture on the wall at a church my parents took us to—it was a picture of Jesus holding a lamb. My dad was a big man that was terrifying, and so I wasn't impressed by Jesus. I didn't see how Jesus could protect me from my father so I didn't see Jesus being helpful. I needed a strong protector.

If God wanted to be important in my life, then why would he hide himself from me? I resented God for years for being elusive. I was deeply hurt—if God was real, why didn't he show himself to me? It was helpful when I realized that God doesn't have a hearing problem...I have a seeing problem.

I couldn't see God working in the world because I had a problem recognizing him. It wasn't that God was hiding so much as I couldn't recognize God when I saw him. My values had to change for me to appreciate God.

I was blinded by my own personal ideas about who God is. I imagined that God was very important and didn't have the time to be dealing with someone as insignificant as me. I had many resentments toward God because I didn't feel worthy of his attention. I couldn't imagine a God different from my father.

How long does it take to undo the damage done by a bad father? I didn't know anything else so it took many years to undo the damage. Abuse leaves a tangled mess that isn't solved overnight.

I was guilty of moving toward ideas that were familiar but not necessarily healthy. The familiar felt safe, so I would cling to ideas that God was cruel in order to protect myself. I didn't like a cruel God, but a cruel God made sense to me.

How would I ever experience anything good if I was going to be defensive most of the time? I was very slow to trust God because the idea of a father was terrifying to me. I had a skewed understanding of who God is.

It took a tremendous amount of courage for me to take a step and trust God—I was very angry at God and I didn't trust him. I wasn't an idiot, so I wasn't going to blindly trust anyone or anything, for that matter.

I decided to build evidence for there being a God. I read books on existential matters ferociously; I watched videos; I went to seminars; I joined a church that was intellectual in its approach to God. I worked very hard for many years to build a bridge to God—I was building my side of the bridge and I was hoping there was a God on the other side building toward me to meet me.

This was a terrifying process because I was devoting all of my time toward something that could turn out to be a fairytale. If it turns out there is no God, then I have wasted my life. The other option was to pursue my own desires and whims for pleasure. I knew in my heart, though, that pursuing my desires would consume me and waste my life. I needed for there to be a God—I didn't want to live a meaningless existence.

I was starved for a meaningful relationship. I felt empty, hopeless, and powerless. I could tell that I was powerless on my own; I needed something inspiring to believe in. I wanted God to be real, but not so badly that I would lobotomize myself and live by blind faith. I had no interest in being a fool.

I needed God to be real. It turns out that many of the impossible questions I had about God could be answered. I stayed honest with myself and did lots of research—I am in a better place because I dared to investigate such impossible claims about Jesus coming back from the dead.

CHAPTER 6

Forgive and Remember

I was relieved when I discovered that Jesus is interested in justice. I had endured a terrible injustice by being an innocent child victimized by child abuse—my heart cried out for justice.

Through mostly hearsay, I understood Jesus to be a pacifist. I heard sermons say to turn the other cheek. The Bible says to turn the other cheek in Matthew 5:39. I had no interest in a God that doesn't believe in justice; I had no interest in following a weak ideology. My father is a violent man. I know violent men exist and they don't care about me. I have to be able to protect myself, and pacifism is a fool's pursuit. A lot of well-meaning, good people are pacifists—I don't believe they have ever been challenged enough to see that pacifism doesn't work.

The famous theologian and anti-Nazi dissident, Dietrich Bonhoeffer, started his life as a pacifist. As the Nazis took power, Dietrich realized that pacifism was not of God and abandoned pacifism to become a part of a plot to assassinate Hitler. Dietrich almost killed Hitler in a bombing. Hitler survived, narrowly escaping the blast. Dietrich was found to be a part of the plot to assassinate Hitler, so he was executed by the Nazis. Dietrich did not take his move to kill Hitler lightly—through much soul-searching, scripture research, and prayer, he came to the conclusion that Hitler must be killed. In hindsight, I believe we can all agree that Hitler was better dead than alive.

The Bible is very clear about it being wrong to take revenge—although, there has been a lot of confusion about what revenge is. Many Christians err on the side of apathy when faced with difficult decisions about justice.

The Bible says, in Leviticus 24:20: "...an eye for an eye." From what I was told, I understood this verse to mean to take revenge. If someone hurts you, then you hurt them back. "An eye for an eye" has been quoted countless times to illustrate revenge.

From what I gathered before I started doing my own research, in the Old Testament was a more vengeful God. When Jesus came to earth in the New Testament, he did away with revenge. I understood that the Old Testament taught revenge and the New Testament taught love.

However, when I started to research and see what the Bible says, it tells a much different story. I have discovered that it's the same God in the Old Testament as the New Testament.

When the Old Testament says "an eye for an eye," it is not referring to revenge. It is, however, referring to justice—it is saying that the punishment shouldn't outweigh the crime; the punishment should be carefully measured to match the crime. It is loving to have a measured response.

The New Testament also says to "turn the other cheek." Is Jesus telling us to ignore justice and be pacifists? Is Jesus telling us to lie down when we are violently attacked? Of course not. I was systematically and violently attacked by my father for years as a child. I was relieved to find that Jesus was not telling me to not seek justice and "forgive and forget."

The NIV Study Bible gives the appropriate cultural context of Matthew 5:39. "Turn the other cheek" has been misinterpreted in our modern context. As I studied "turn the other cheek," I found that it is only referring to insults. In the Old Testament a person would slap someone on the cheek as a way of insulting them—it was not considered assault. A slap on the cheek was considered more of an insult than an act of violence.

It is correct to say we are commanded to not seek justice when we are verbally provoked. It is true to say we should endure insults with no retaliation.

The verse "turn the other cheek" has been misused when it is applied to physical assault as defined in our current culture. In modern times this verse has been misused to tell people who have been physically assaulted to not seek justice because that's what God would want. They wrongfully refer to Matthew 5:39, "turn the other cheek," as proof that God doesn't approve of seeking justice or self-defense.

I am a victim of violent child abuse. Jesus is telling me not to take revenge, yet I am to pursue justice. What a relief—Jesus is fighting for me. I find great comfort in knowing that God hates when his children are hurt unfairly. God hates child abuse; Jesus is fighting for me.

It's my job to set boundaries with evil people and bring justice wherever and whenever I can. I am to resist revenge and double-down on justice. I am to confront my abuser if it's safe. I am to do everything in my power to keep from such a terrible crime happening again. I hold my abusers accountable and expose their lies. I proclaim my innocence in the city street. I fight with every ounce of my energy against the condemning accusations my abuser has brought against me.

Justice means that I am to go through the proper channels when seeking restitution. Seeking justice ensures that I have a proper response. Seeking justice is loving my enemies. We should seek justice because mankind is made in the image of God—every individual has infinite value. Seeking justice is loving yourself and loving your enemy.

I learned about the true definition of forgiveness—most people believe that forgiveness means to forgive-and-forget. Many falsely believe that forgiveness means you don't seek justice. Not true. I am to forgive my abusers but I should never forget; forgetting sets me up to be abused again. I forgive and set up boundaries so it never happens again. I am to hold people accountable when they hurt me.

Forgiveness ensures that I do not fall victim to evil myself. It ensures that I do not take revenge. Forgiveness ensures that I have a measured response—a fair response. Revenge is arrogant and dangerous. Revenge requires no thought and overreacts; a fool takes revenge.

A wise man seeks justice so he doesn't destroy himself in the process of trying to protect himself. Forgiveness *never* lets the abuser off the hook. Forgiveness holds the abuser accountable. When forgiveness is done with wisdom, the abuser is exposed.

The abuser can hide behind revenge—there is no accountability for the abuser with revenge. Forgiveness ensures you remain blameless and pure. Your forgiveness is a light that exposes what's in the darkness. Forgiveness protects me from becoming like my abuser. Forgiveness is a calculating response that helps you to keep a clear head so you are able to expose the crime.

The weak forgive-and-forget. The strong forgive-and-remember—not seeking revenge, but building a boundary so the crimes never happen again. Forgive-and-remember takes your abuser to task and holds them accountable before God and mankind.

God is the ultimate judge. Luke 6:37 says: "Do not judge, and you will not be judged. Do not condemn, and you will not be condemned. Forgive and you will be forgiven." This verse is God telling us to stay out of the way when he judges evil people; this verse is telling us that God is real and we should consider him in our response to evil. God is warning us that we will be hurt if we do not let him go first. If I don't let God go first, then I will be overwhelmed by evil.

I am not to live as if there is no God—I am not strong enough to take on evil alone. Hebrews 3:13 says, "But encourage one another daily. As long as it is called today, so that none of you may be hardened by sin's deceitfulness." Sin can be seductive. Do not let sin trick you into revenge.

God is warning us to stay out of the way of the blast when he deals with your abusers. God is real and he will hold evil people accountable. I don't want to be anywhere near evil people when God's wrath falls. God is patient and when he brings judgment, it is devastating.

I am a child of God, the son of the living king—I have all the rights therein. I fight with a righteous anger against evil. I accepted Christ as my king; my pedigree would have it no other way. I will confront evil wherever I find it.

Jesus Christ suffered and died on a cross in order to give me a choice. I choose justice. I choose strength. I choose love.

CHAPTER 7

LOVING MY ENEMIES

It can be a lonely road pursuing love for one's enemies—love requires me to confront relationship problems and to take initiative when I see a problem. I was told by the church culture that Jesus is most interested in everyone getting along. I understood that Jesus is most interested in everyone being nice to each other—that is not true. Jesus wants us to be kind to each other but never to ignore evil as a means of avoiding conflict.

Now, I understand that Jesus doesn't tolerate evil—Jesus hates evil. I should hate evil also. When I started hating evil, I became a problem for people wanting to do evil. Matthew 10:34-39 says, "I did not come to bring peace, but a sword. I have come so that a son will be against his father, a daughter will be against her mother, a daughter-in-law will be against her mother-in-law. A person's enemies will be members of his own family."

Jesus is not against family here—Jesus loves family. Jesus is saying that not even family relationships are immune from justice; he is saying how seriously he takes evil. Unfortunately, much evil is manifested in families. As I followed Jesus, it challenged all of the relationships I was in. I had to choose between getting along or speaking out against injustice. I had to speak up for myself, even if it meant losing those closest to me. What a terrible but necessary choice.

Jesus calls me his child—I am his now. I have been grafted into Christ's family. I had no choice over my earthly family, but I have been given a choice to be in the line of Christ by his death and resurrection from the dead. I am now a child of God, so I should behave like a child of God. I will be like Jesus and fight for the weak and protect the innocent. I will also fight for myself.

I will suffer persecution, like Christ, when I speak out against evil. I have chosen the more difficult road that brings a much greater reward. The greater reward is for me to be able to look in the mirror and love what I see—I love myself because God loves me.

Jesus was killed by men because he is good. Christians will also be attacked simply because they want to make the world a better place—this is called persecution. I have been heavily persecuted at times because I decided to take responsibility for myself.

If a person decides to take responsibility for themselves, then they will cause problems for all irresponsible people around them. Most people, I find, are being morally irresponsible in some way. Most people are so wrapped up in their wicked ways that they have a great deal of resentment and hate for Jesus followers. Truth works like a bright light—as I fell in love with truth, it began to bring light into dark places. I loved the light and how it brought sanity to my world. I ran into problems with the people around me that love the darkness; people that prefer chaos fought against me.

More specifically, people are medicating their own pain by believing lies. They prefer the darkness because they are running from their own conscience and the light reveals their limitations. People prefer to hide their character defects with lies and deceit. I found myself running into a great deal of resistance from my family and friends as I started taking responsibility for myself and stopped enabling their bad behavior. I had stepped out of the darkness and become light. I made enemies overnight from those that prefer the darkness. I became public enemy number one to many people that I loved dearly.

I shared my excitement for the truth—I shared compelling reasons why it's better to confront the hurts in our lives. I argued to try and convince those around me that it's better to live truthfully. I was able to stand my ground; I was satisfied with my efforts.

I was met with a great deal of resistance. I noticed that when they couldn't win against my arguments, they began to attack my character—I was accused of being a troublemaker. My credibility and reputation were attacked. I learned that if people can't win the arguments, they will often resort to attacking the person's character. I met with the persecution that Jesus warned me about. It was a ruthless onslaught; it was devastating; it broke my heart. I lost many people that I dearly loved.

CHAPTER 8

LIVE MY BEST LIFE

In my search for truth, I eventually got a master's degree in psychology. I had immersed myself so much in finding answers, that getting a master's degree was naturally the next step. I am a seeker; I am desperate to live the best life a person can live. I want to compensate for all the years lost to child abuse.

I believe that the abuse had left me with a nagging sense of meaninglessness in my heart—I had no stomach for doing the traditional things to find happiness. I had no interest in the normal things people would strive for. I saw people all around me striving for materialism, family, money, etc. I also saw that the people all around me were unhappy—that was coupled with the belief that I would never know happiness because of what my father said about me. I saw myself as hopeless. I lived life moment to moment; I didn't have the ability to plan for the future because I was using most of my strength to survive day to day.

One of the ways I found to cope was to write in a journal. I found myself writing often—it helped with the pain. Writing enabled me to take the chaos in my head and organize it into coherent thoughts. I could take what was invisible and make it visible; I could organize my thoughts, in time and space, with a paper and pen in front of me.

While getting my undergraduate degree, I started reading books about meaning and purpose. I searched out books that spoke to me. I wanted to figure out how to overcome my weaknesses—I wanted to find hope. I was getting an undergraduate degree in journalism because my strength was in writing. At the time, I had no idea that writing was a strength of mine—I was confused and doing what came easiest for me.

I had no money to my name. I was able to go to college because college was big business. The colleges got rich from enrolling students. The schools wanted students, so they found grants and loans for me to attend. The school had no problem putting me in debt so I could attend. At the time, all I heard was that to be somebody you needed to go to college—I went to college because I didn't want to feel left out. I had no plan when I went to college.

Mostly I forced my way through my undergraduate degree. I filled myself with impossible goals to offset the mind-bending terror of helplessness and hopelessness that assailed me daily. I would get trashed on alcohol weekly to numb the pain from feeling lost; getting wasted on alcohol gave me the temporary peace I needed to cope. Most of the time I felt like an impostor, faking my way through a world of brilliant people. Being wasted raised me up for a moment to speak with the worthy people—the people that actually mattered; that is how I thought at the time, but not anymore.

CHAPTER 9

Gentle Jesus

In my search to decide if God is real, I joined a church. I found a church that I appreciated because the pastor was interested in intellectual pursuits. I was told to repent by the leadership. It was explained to me that repentance is the act of turning away from my sins. I was told that repentance means to stand up and turn 180 degrees away from my sins and walk away. I found myself repenting quite often because I would return inevitably back to the addictive behaviors I had. After awhile, repentance actually became humiliating because I couldn't stop my addictive behavior—it simply didn't work.

I was in too much pain and I didn't trust Jesus enough to believe he would catch me when I fell. For years I would be in a cycle. The cycle went like this: I would be hurting tremendously, then I would turn to the addiction for relief; next I would feel humiliated and ashamed; then I would go back to resisting the urge to sin. I understood repentance to mean that I would white-knuckle my way through overwhelming desires to medicate my pain. Each time I failed...I would try harder the next time. I was told a bad definition of repentance by well-meaning church leaders.

Through religious rhetoric, I was told to fight temptation with my own power, not by calling on Christ's power.

In time, I came to understand a better definition of what it means to repent. I now understand repentance as living life on your knees. I am not supposed to overcome temptation on my own. I used to pray: "I confess my sins to you, Lord; now I promise to try harder." Now I pray: "God, I don't have the strength to defeat temptation; I surrender to you and ask for your help."

I am to express my remorse, confess trying to do life on my terms, and live daily in humility to God's guidance. I pray for God to lead me and I resist the urge to run ahead of him. When I can't resist a temptation and I find myself running to do that desire, I am to treat myself the way Jesus treats me—with gentleness.

The Bible says in Romans 5:8, "But God proves his love for us in this: While we were still sinners, Christ died for us." If Christ suffered and died for us when we didn't even know him, how understanding is he when we sin against him as his children? Jesus understands us.

God came to earth in the form of Jesus. He became a human. He understands what it is like to be in great pain and to have the desire to do anything to make that pain go away.

Jesus doesn't expect us to be perfect, but he does expect us to take responsibility for when we hurt someone. Submitting to Jesus is simply taking responsibility for our human nature, which is to be selfish and deceitful.

Every moment, Jesus is ready to pour his great mercy and love onto us—to receive that mercy, we are to live surrendered lives on our knees before him. We are to let Jesus lead as we enjoy the adventure he has put in front of us.

I believe Jesus doesn't want us to feel bad; Jesus wants us to feel good. Jesus gave us a way out of the condemnation of our sins through repentance. Jesus is not looking to make us suffer, because he already suffered in our place on the cross. I am hurting myself when I sin—Jesus is the solution.

I find a great deal of comfort in what Jesus said. In Matthew 11:28-30, Jesus said, "Come to me all who labor and are heavy laden, and I will give you rest. Take my yoke upon you, and learn from me; for I am gentle and lowly in heart, and you will find rest for your souls. For my yoke is easy and my burden is light."

The prophet Isaiah said this about Jesus, mentioned in Matthew 12:20: "A bruised reed he will not break, and a smoldering wick he will not extinguish, till he leads justice to victory." A bruised reed and a smoldering wick are fragile. Jesus will take great care with those who are wounded. I find that, sometimes, I am much harder on myself for sinning than Jesus is—sometimes I will punish myself out of guilt; Jesus wants no part of that.

Jesus is gentle. He wants to teach us his gentleness so we will be gentle with ourselves. Jesus is gentle with the abused, so I should be gentle with myself as well. I didn't do anything wrong to deserve child abuse—I should treat myself accordingly.

CHAPTER 10

FALL IN LOVE WITH JESUS

Be careful not to confuse repentance for penance—repentance is to surrender yourself to God's ways; penance is voluntary self-punishment, inflicted as an outward expression of repentance for doing wrong. Many well-meaning leaders in the church confuse repentance for penance.

Originally, the word "penance" simply means the desire to be forgiven. Although penance has been abused to mean a person making themselves right before God, through their own efforts—like many words, its original meaning has been abused.

Fake penance is not of God. It is man's efforts to make himself clean before God. It is wrong because it dishonors what Jesus Christ did at the cross. Jesus was tortured and killed horribly to rescue us from trying to save ourselves—Jesus paid a heavy price; we should not dishonor his sacrifice by assuming we can do anything to save ourselves. Fake penance looks and feels spiritual, but it is a lie.

When a person tries to quit an addiction or a sinful behavior and they use their own strength to stop sinning, it simply doesn't work. Addictions and sins we cannot stop are meant to drive us to our knees *and keep us there*. We are to live life on our knees.

We are to learn from our addictions, not only stop the behavior. Jesus doesn't usually take our addictive behavior away all at once, because we need to learn how to live life on our knees.

If God took a person's addictions away all at once, then they would go on living a lifestyle that contradicts what God wants for us. Too often people are content with believing life doesn't get any better than their best memory—God wants to give us new and better memories. Unbreakable sin patterns are there to help us to change our values; values are not changed overnight.

I believe that God is more interested in changing our perspective on sin than to get us to quit sinning. Jesus understands that we live in a world where we can't escape sin. Jesus isn't wringing his hands in frustration with his children who are caught in patterns of sin; he knows we will always be sinning as long as we are alive on this side of heaven. Jesus is hoping our sin will drive us to a place where we give up on doing life under our own strength and begin to rely on God's strength.

Jesus weeps when we hurt and he is happy when we feel good—all of the things people are addicted to are not bad things; they only become bad when they are abused. God wants us to begin to get obsessed with him, not our addictions. Over the years, as Jesus has shown himself reliable, I have fallen in love with him—there is no greater obsession than love. Now, I must keep watch over my heart so it is not stolen away by a lesser god.

In 2 Corinthians 12:5-10, the apostle Paul said that he was given a thorn in his flesh to keep him from becoming conceited. Paul begged God to remove the thorn, but God did not remove it, so as to help Paul to remember to live life on his knees before God. I believe God removes many temptations, yet some are not removed because it helps us to live our best life.

Trust isn't won overnight—it takes time to build trust. We must learn to trust Jesus more than our addictions. It takes many years to change one's values; it takes many years to build a strong relationship with Jesus. Don't quit before the miracle happens—keep returning to Jesus each time you fail and never give up. Learn to live life on your knees. Learn how to live a surrendered life. Get to know Jesus; give him a chance. Jesus has something far better for you. Don't be content with fleeting pleasures and a mediocre life—fall in love with Jesus. Learn to love him more than sin; this can be done in time—you won't regret it.

CHAPTER 11

TRUST

I believe in God because he has given me a life worth living. I never understood the word "faith" until much later in my walk with God—I could have given a correct definition of faith; even so, I did not understand it. My head knew how to define faith, yet my heart did not understand.

In the beginning I saw myself as the sum of my experiences and nothing more. I didn't see God as something I could turn to because I believed God was an impossible concept to understand. I saw myself as condemned because of my limited experience and lack of talents. In my mind, I wasn't born with any of the skills or talents needed to be successful in the world; I wasn't as lucky as most people around me. I felt condemned by my lack of luck and experience in the gene pool.

It was terrifying to start moving toward the idea that there could be a God. I was scared because I could be following the tooth fairy for all I knew. "Finding God" seemed impossible, and I felt humiliated by my desperate need to be rescued. I was desperate, though, and desperate people do desperate things—I decided to trust in the idea that there is a God and to believe he is good.

I felt if there is a God, then he has a lot of explaining to do. Why would God be so cruel as to let me suffer under so much injustice? I was an abused child—you don't get more innocent than that.

My experience was telling me that there is no good God. I had witnessed that evil is much stronger than good. My experience was one of being saturated and overwhelmed by evil. I thought, if there is good out there…it is terribly weak and useless.

Faith is the same as trust. The only thing that could break me out of this worldview that evil is stronger than good is faith—I had to believe something different; I had to believe that good is stronger than evil. I had to trust in a total stranger. I had to trust in this far-fetched magical notion that a man that called himself God, over two thousand years ago, could help me today. I felt foolish and also terrified because I didn't want to be hurt any more than I already was. It took a tremendous amount of hope for me to take a tiny step forward under God's care. Jesus says in Matthew 17:20: "He replied, 'Because you have so little faith. Truly I tell you, if you have faith as small as a mustard seed, you can say to this mountain, "Move from here to there," and it will move. Nothing will be impossible for you.'" Mustard seeds are tiny—it's amazing that they grow into anything. The seeds are usually about one to two millimeters in diameter.

Almost everything in me was saying that God couldn't be real. As much as the pain of living helpless and hopeless is…hope is also a very painful exercise; exercising hope felt like I was setting myself up to be humiliated and hurt further. I was terrified that the universe was going to play another joke on me and leave me even more isolated and alone than when I started.

My desire for justice drove me to take up my faith. Someone hurt me really bad, and I wanted them to be held accountable. I didn't want revenge because I could see that revenge would destroy me in the process of making my abusers pay. I set my sights on justice—the best "revenge" is for me to become happy and successful.

I stepped out and decided to trust Jesus and what he said. In my heart I wanted my abusers and my siblings to, one day, be reunited under love. I wanted us all laughing together and being happy together.

The only way for me to change my views about evil being more powerful than good was for me to live as if good were stronger and see what came of that. One thing that helped me was to stop running from pain and to start running toward Jesus. I was running aimlessly to escape pain in the beginning. Jesus gave me focus and purpose—I went from running aimlessly from pain to running toward Jesus.

Through faith in Jesus, I started doing new things—things that were out of character for me. One example was going to church—going to church wasn't something that I identified with at all. After committing myself to church, I also joined a discipleship group, and eventually this led to joining a Christian recovery group. The whole time I was assailed in doubt. I was in a tremendous amount of pain from hoping and doubting—it was all terrifying. As scary as everything was…the scariest thing to me was losing my sanity from chaos. Chaos was the most painful thing I had experienced.

Both hope and hopelessness are painful. Hopelessness is a knife that cuts indiscriminately, without purpose. Hope is also a knife, yet it cuts with a surgeon's precision. Hope cut the diseased ideology from my mind. Hope is painful, but living hopeless is unbearable.

Faith took me outside myself; trust in Jesus enabled me to escape the rotten ideologies that held me captive. Through faith, I was able to take measured risks that were reasonable.

It was never blind faith—blind faith is for fools. Jesus never asked me to take a blind leap—I wouldn't have done that anyway;

I always did a tremendous amount of research before I would take a risk. There is "risk" and then there is "risky." I learned the difference between risk and risky: it was a risk to follow Jesus but never risky. "Risk" is a measured response; "risky" is a blind leap without looking. Faith never asks one to take a blind leap. I did my homework.

CHAPTER 12

Be Humble

In the beginning, I was never interested in church. I saw Christians as people who were trying to be good. Being good was never interesting to me because I saw good people as weak people; I didn't want to be evil, but I also didn't want to be too good either. I wanted to be a good man, but more than that, I wanted to feel safe. My idea of being "good" was a person that avoided confrontation at all cost—I knew that one couldn't avoid confrontation without being weak. I had no interest in being weak.

I met many well-meaning Christians who saw themselves as good people. My experience with people who thought of themselves as good had been that they were mostly weak people because they were more interested in getting along with others than telling the truth. Truth sets one apart from others. Truth can be offensive to those who are more interested in tolerance than justice. I found good people who were more interested in conforming me to their beliefs than being a good listener. One should seek to understand before being understood.

As I studied more about Jesus, I realized that Jesus wasn't interested in good people as much as he was interested in humble people. A good man can end up in hell. No one can be good enough, according to scripture. Romans 3:23 says, "For all have sinned and fall short of the glory of God." I knew I could never be good enough, so I felt condemned by the idea of being good.

Being good and being nice were synonymous to me—both being good and being nice would get you hurt because it makes you unsafe by being a target for predators. I never admired anyone who seemed weak to me—I wanted to be strong.

In Genesis 2, God instructed Adam and Eve not to eat from the tree of good and evil. The tree was made up of good and evil. Being good can get you into just as much trouble as being evil. I like the saying: "The road to hell is paved with good intentions." I can have the best intentions, but if I don't present those intentions to God in prayer, I can do a lot of damage. Selfish ambition always looks "good" to the one that it benefits. Good is relative if it is pursued without accountability to God.

I no longer look to do what is good or right. I now look to do the "loving" thing. It is better to do the loving thing rather than the right thing. I can have the right response, yet still be wrong because it isn't the loving response. One is in danger of not being a help if their ego and pride is engaged rather than their empathy. Empathy is the loving response. Empathy engages the whole self. 1 Corinthians 13:1-3:

If I speak in the tongues of men and of angels, but have not love, I am only a ringing gong or a clanging cymbal. If I have the gift of prophecy and can fathom all mysteries and all knowledge, and I have absolute faith as to move mountains, but have not love, I am nothing. If I give all I possess to the poor and exult in the surrender of my body, but have not love, I gain nothing.

I believe most people know the difference between right and wrong, so we don't need someone reminding us to be good. If a believer has a weak moment and gives into sin, most of the time they know they did wrong—most sins aren't done out of ignorance but out of weakness. Telling a recovering alcoholic that he shouldn't have gone to the bar the night before and gotten drunk is not helpful. It is "right" that they shouldn't have gone to the bar, but it is not helpful to say that.

The "right" response says: "You shouldn't have gone to the bar last night." The "loving" response says: "I am sorry you went to the bar last night." Trying to give the right response is a person who is more interested in raising themselves up; giving a loving response is a person who is more interested in lifting the other person up. I have found that people are more interested in feeling like I care rather than hearing me tell them what to do. In our hearts we know right from wrong. What we need is an understanding person to show us that we are loved. Loneliness is the killer. Empathy says to the other person that they are not alone. Intimacy in human connection is what the heart desires most. When a struggling person feels understood then they have the fuel to continue to fight against their enemies.

Many good people will end up in hell because they refused to submit to their creator. "Good" people who end up in hell were only being good for selfish reasons. They were trying to raise themselves up over others. These people give the appearance of being good, yet on the inside, they are corrupt. Jesus said in Matthew 23:26: "You clean the outside of the cup and dish, but inside they are full of greed and self-indulgence. Blind Pharisee! First clean the inside of the cup and dish, and then the outside will also be clean."

I knew I could never be good enough to get into heaven. I could tell that I didn't have what it takes to be good enough. I was glad to see that Jesus didn't give favoritism to good people. I was glad to see that Jesus doesn't give favoritism to anybody.

I fell in love with Jesus when I saw that he judged people by their heart and not by the amount of good they had done. Jesus loves the rebellious people and the legalistic people equally. Jesus is beautiful—these new understandings helped me to fall in love with Jesus.

CHAPTER 13

Moral Compass

The Christian and the non-Christian are at the mercy of the same brutal world; we are both assailed by the same problems of pain and suffering—what Christianity has to offer is a different perspective on the world. I was indoctrinated from my youth that the natural world was brought about by accident. Random things happened and here I am today. The outcome from randomness is meaninglessness.

According to many well-meaning scientists that don't believe in God, the world is a brutal place where the only law is survival-of-the-fittest. They say the world is a random place and that humans are the same as animals. It is easy to believe such ideas because the world can be very brutal. It was easy for me to believe, in the beginning, because I was jaded by my introduction to this world. I entered a world of savagery when I was born; I had no reason to believe the world isn't random and cruel.

As I began to search for meaning, though, I could not deny the beautiful things of the world. I was full of despair, while at the same time, I was full of a powerful desire to experience beauty and joy. My heart ached to experience something that would help me forget that I lived in a world devoid of meaning. I was terrified of the reality that the world is a brutal place, devoid of meaning. I overcompensated for this fear of meaninglessness with a powerful enthusiasm to create something out of nothing. I became ambitious toward the things that I thought would give me meaning in a meaningless world.

Meaninglessness chased me like a horrible banshee into ambitious projects—projects designed to lift me up above the lonely despair humanity had found themselves in. I was swimming upstream in a torrent of meaninglessness, knowing that one day my strength would fail and I would be washed away into the gutter of history to be forgotten.

I began to study another perspective on the world. I looked into the idea of there being a God. I told myself that I would abandon this idea of God the moment I could prove there was no God. I researched God because I was being honest in my studies. I hadn't seen God disproved, so I had to consider there could be something at work in the bigger picture.

On one hand, I had very intelligent people telling me that humans came about by accident. On the other hand, I had religious people telling me we were created by a creator. I thought the people that said there was a God needed to divorce themselves from reason to believe such things. As I examined the credentials and authority of the religious people, I found that they were no different in their intellect than the nonbelievers—the Christians had graduated from many of the same universities as the atheists.

I noticed a trend with the scientists. The atheistic scientists would not consider the idea of there being a God at all, whereas the honest Christian scientists would investigate the science that presumed there was no God. The Christians had a fearlessness that the atheists did not have—I could see that the scientists who were Christian were unfairly being marginalized simply because they believed in God.

I find atheism to be presumptuous in a world where the existence of God has not been disproved. No one can prove that God does not exist—believing or not believing in God has no effect on science. Science stands alone. Math is the same for an atheist as it is for the Christian. Both parties can stay true to math while believing in two totally different ideologies. I find that atheists bully Christians because of what they believe. I don't find scientists who are Christians bullying atheists near as much as the latter.

Atheists in the mainstream scientific community have been bullying me with fear for most of my life. The origin of life, macro-evolution, and anthropogenic global warming have been presented as scientific facts. In truth, these are scientific *theories*, not facts. A scientific theory is simply an educated guess; an educated guess is simply a guess. Mainstream scientists are giving their best guess and presenting it as facts. They can guess the science much better than me because of their skill and training, but it is still a guess. Scientific theory is scientific guessing. In recent times, scientists have been given too much authority to dictate how we should live our lives. Mainstream scientists have become cult leaders in many circles.

I find the mainstream scientific community has become a religious cult. They now have become dogmatic in their beliefs and their "facts" can be called orthodoxy. They will punish anyone who has an alternative scientific belief with public humiliation and excommunication from their elite circles. The atheistic scientific community has become pseudoscience—it is a cult.

On the origin of life, mainstream science has been saying that life on Earth comes from a single cell. They claim that life started as a simple form and became complex over time—over billions of years, life went from simple to complex.

New scientific discovery has shown this to be false. The cell is a vastly complex organism that could never have been simple. Life has not been evolving from one species to another. The atheists believe in macroevolution. Macroevolution says that the "species" of animals have been evolving into new species over time. They are saying a lizard has become a bird or an ape has become a man.

On the other hand, microevolution says that evolution only happens within a particular species. Microevolution says there is no evidence that one particular species can change into another and claims that variations happen only within species. For example: Birds have different variations of beaks within one species of bird. Microevolution says evolution is only present when a species changes characteristics to adapt to its environment. An example is where they found the same species of bird across the world, yet the birds' beaks were shaped differently from each region they were found. The birds' beaks had changed shape to adapt to the environment they were in—there is a huge difference between beaks changing shape and a lizard becoming a bird.

Mainstream science claims they have settled the issue on the origin of life. World-renowned chemist, Dr. James Tour, is a believer in Jesus Christ. Dr. James Tour proves that the origin of life has not been settled, as the atheists have said. Dr. James Tour is exposing the lies and corruption of mainstream science. The book *The Mystery of Life's Origin: The Continuing Controversy* is an excellent source if you are interested in going further in depth on the origin of life.

Anthropogenic global warming is another method mainstream science uses to bully people. Anthropogenic simply means man-made. Global warming has become a religion as well. I like the term "climate alarmist" to identify those that would take the subject of global warming and use it to spread terror among the population. Climate alarmists are part of a doomsday cult that is a trillion-dollar industry. Fortunes can be made from selling fear. The problems with the climate have been overexaggerated to the point of hysteria. From what I have learned, the earth has had cooling trends and warming trends from the beginning.

German physicist and meteorologist, Klaus-Eckart Puls, looked into the claims of the climate alarmists about man-made global warming. Klaus-Eckart Puls said:

Ten years ago I simply parroted what the IPCC (Intergovernmental Panel on Climate Change) told us. One day I started checking the facts and data—first I started with a sense of doubt, but then I became outraged when I discovered that much of what the IPCC and the media were telling us was sheer nonsense and was not even supported by any scientific facts and measurements. To this day I still feel shame that, as a scientist, I made presentations of their science without first checking it...scientifically, it is sheer absurdity to think we can get a nice climate by turning a CO_2 adjustment knob.

In the book *Human Caused Global Warming*, Dr. Tim Ball calls man-made global

warming "the biggest deception in history."

I have found mainstream science has become a fear-mongering doomsday cult. They are negative and not scientifically sound; most of what I have been taught on scientific issues I learned in public school.

My relationship with Jesus Christ enabled me to become an independent thinker. The message of Jesus Christ empowers the individual as a wonderful, intelligent creation with infinite value. My mind is a space that many ideologies and beliefs try to forcibly occupy. As I learned that I am valuable, I began to fight for myself. I no longer tolerated bullies. I began to challenge popular thought.

Tyrannical governments always move to eradicate Christianity. Jesus Christ was killed as a political revolutionary. America's exceptionalism comes from its Judeo-Christian roots. Freedom always follows a people that turn to Jesus Christ. Tyrants do not want their population believing they are special. Tyrants will not tolerate another Lord in their midst—tyrants want us broken and easily managed.

I do not pretend to be a scientific expert on anything. I have learned to navigate most fields by using my feelings *and* my rational mind together. I have learned to use my feelings to detect lies. If I find that I am starting to become too fearful, I remember what my God says in Isaiah 41:10: "So do not fear, for I am with you; do not be dismayed, for I am your God. I will strengthen you and help you; I will uphold you with my righteous right hand."

When I feel afraid, I am alerted that something is wrong. I use the fear as an alarm to tell me when I need to pay closer attention to what I am doing. I may not understand a subject, but my fear warns me to be cautious. My fear is warning me. I have learned to discern a subject by doing lots of research.

We live in a day where the "experts" have let us down. The scientific experts have been found to be corrupt. The government experts have become corrupt, so I must learn how to find the information I need to survive.

Believing in God has given me a conscience. I now use that conscience to navigate many topics that I don't understand. My conscience speaks to me; my instincts are sharper now that I have a moral center in my life. I have become moral, and morality has a wonderful way of detecting lies and corruption. I not only look at "facts" from the experts, but I have also learned to look at character. I never saw character as a means to detecting a con artist in the past.

When I became a follower of Jesus Christ, my character began to develop. Building my character has built my discernment. I used to look only at the facts when judging an expert—I believed that what a person does with their personal life has no bearing on their professional life. I have found that not to be true. I have learned to look at a person's character as well as their credentials; what a person does in their personal life directly impacts their professional life.

I would only look at a person's credentials in the past—I was only getting half the story. Now I spot a true expert by looking at both their credentials and their personal life. I do not have to be knowledgeable in a field to spot a person who knows what they are doing.

In time, with patience, I will be able to find the expert through trial and error. If the expert I find has amazing credentials but I find him lying regularly to me, then I need to ditch this expert, no matter how amazing their credentials. I would rather have a less experienced, honest person than a corrupt genius—the corrupt genius is impressive, but he will likely rip me off. The honest person will make honest mistakes, but they will stay to finish what they started. The humble and honest novice will never try to hurt me; the corrupt genius will find a way to manipulate me for their own gain.

I use my moral judgment to help navigate politics or science. Morality only comes from God. An atheist can claim morality, but they are borrowing from Christianity when they do this. There is no moral right and wrong for an atheist—morality is a spiritual concept. Morals are where we find what is right and wrong; it is how laws are made. If we have laws, then there must be a law-giver. The only law-giver can be God.

I have learned how to hold my abusers accountable when I turned to God for help. God helped me understand right from wrong. I have a moral compass because I believe in God; I can measure a person's character now.

Pure science can stand on its own—it's the scientist that can be corrupt. Applying morality to scientists is how I find the expert I will rely on. No one is unbiased; there has never been an unbiased theory. A humble, honest scientist understands that scientific discoveries are never closed—everything is always open to interpretation. Science is always changing; God stays the same. Jesus Christ is a reliable worldview.

CHAPTER 14

BEAUTIFUL WORLD

When I look around the world, I can't help but see beauty, love, and charity. I see that humans have both charity and evil. It's easy to get overwhelmed by the evil and adopt a worldview of despair; however, adopting despair is dishonest—there is good in the world. It seems very small at times, but I would be lying to myself if I ever decided to believe that beauty didn't exist. I believe beauty comes from God because it defies the cold dark void. Things keep dying; however, things keep being born.

Life contradicts death the same as death contradicts life. I have decided to accept both realities. Accepting both realities requires me to take a spiritual leap—I don't believe there is any other way to remain intellectually honest than to accept that both life and death are equally happening at the same time.

I find that when I try to accept death as natural, then everything that is good in me goes to war against that idea. I find when I try to focus only on life, then death haunts me like a ghost. How do I solve this dilemma? The Christian worldview.

The best explanation to me is that we are living in a world that is fallen, where humans are being punished. When I look around the world, I see a beautiful creation antagonized by destructive forces. Evil itself tends to work like rust or decay. I believe that rust and decay cannot exist without life; however, life can exist without rust and decay. Life defines death, yet death cannot define life. Death is the antithesis of all things. Death in itself is nothing, whereas life in itself is wholeness.

My heart yearns for wholeness; my heart yearns for relationship and life. The only times I yearn for death is in despair. I never yearn for death when I am full of life. Death is clearly a disease. I believe death is a curse. Humans have been sentenced to death by a judge. I believe there is evidence of heaven all around us in beauty and love; however, there is also strong evidence that everything good is under a curse—that makes sense to me.

I believe that people who don't believe in Jesus are guilty of pessimism. To believe in anything other than Jesus is to accept defeat, in my mind. Jesus said in John 10:10: "The thief comes only to steal and kill and destroy; I have come that they may have life, and have it to the full." I haven't found anything, scientifically or otherwise, that proves Jesus didn't exist. To the contrary, I find a great deal of evidence that Jesus existed.

I can look at death through the perspective of fear. I find looking at death through fear is like looking at death through death's eyes. Fear isn't helpful at all. I find it more satisfying to embrace the likeliness that death is an intruder. Death feels like an intruder—it feels wrong; life feels right.

I find plenty of intellectual evidence for Jesus; at the same time, my heart believes Jesus to be true. My heart feels good when it believes in life. I have learned not to rely on anything unless *both* my *head* and my *heart* come together on the issue. I find I have good discernment when I align good reasoning with peaceful feelings. My head and my heart both work together to make sense of my world.

I can believe something intellectually; however, my heart won't accept it. I can believe something with my heart, although my head won't accept it. My mind can deceive me and my heart can deceive me—when my head and heart align, I move forward. My head and heart come together on the subject of Jesus.

When I look at the world as "survival of the fittest," my perspective becomes pessimistic and negative; I feel that death is telling me how to live. When I look at the world through love—which is the act of God sending his son to die on a cross to reunite people with their creator—my perspective becomes one of hope and love. I believe in hope and love. I didn't used to believe in hope and love, but I never gave up. I didn't quit prematurely.

I chose to be honest with myself and look to see if God exists. I didn't understand it at the time, but now I see that my effort to look for God was an act of love toward God himself. I believe God was pleased because he rewarded me. God has rewarded me by overwhelming the evil in my life with good. I still have some painful things that haven't changed, yet God has given me a life worth living.

In my journey seeking God—which brought me outside myself—I have been introduced to new ways of living that sustain me. My trusting God has rewarded me with fulfilling relationships. I never dreamed that I would have a wife who admires me and a daughter who wants to be around me. My love for God has translated into my bringing happiness to the world for those around me. I have experienced real change for good.

God has been training me through faith. No longer do I seek instant gratification as a means to survive. My ability to learn and adapt to my environment has grown exponentially. I have learned to wait on the edge of the abyss for an invisible God. My patience has been rewarded with a beautiful family and wisdom to navigate the perils of life. I have been given a new and better perspective to deal with my current situation that seems impossible.

I have found that God has revealed himself to me because I searched for him. In John 14:21, Jesus said, "Whoever has my commandments and keeps them is the one who loves me. The one who loves me will be loved by my father, and I will love him and reveal myself to him." Jesus has revealed himself to me through many precious ways. In hindsight I can see that my daughter was born the same time that I came to believe that I am valuable beyond belief. God has been rewarding my faith in him with things I never valued in the past. Jesus has been changing my values.

Many of the things that made me feel good in the past are not the same things that I turn to today to feel good. I was hopeless and believed life was meaningless in the past. I believe, today, that life is worth living—God gave me new desires in my heart; healthy desires.

CHAPTER 15

BE OBSESSED WITH JESUS

I had a realization during my search that whatever I loved had two sides. On one hand, what I loved gave me great pleasure; on the other hand, what I loved gave me great pain. I found that whatever I loved came with limitations—I was subject to those limitations by my devotion.

The Bible refers to these loves as idols. I was looking for something to be inspired by; I was looking for something to give me passion.

I looked for happiness in my relationship with my girlfriend. She was my inspiration that was going to help me be all that I could be. I saw her as the answer to my crushing feelings of loneliness; I was flattered by her attention.

I believed that if she saw me as attractive, then that must mean I am valuable. I found myself trying to glean value from my relationship with her. I was mostly frustrated because I never believed that I was lovable. I still tried to find significance in the relationship; however, I kept running into my own inability to receive love. I couldn't receive love because deep in my heart, I believed I was unlovable. I was on a roller coaster of hope and despair as I did my best to fix the problems in our relationship.

I had made my girlfriend an idol because I believed that our relationship was the key to happiness. In the beginning of the relationship I was wonderfully smitten by her—it felt euphoric to be lost in a powerful obsession that gave me meaning and life. As time went on, though, things started coming apart. I was in denial for many years that I was losing inspiration in the relationship. A deep despair crept in over time. I was devastated. I lived in quiet desperation trying to salvage our relationship. I must have exasperated that poor girl. I am happy she stayed with me through it all.

I found myself having a pattern of getting obsessed about something, then becoming disappointed, and then falling into despair. It was exasperating—I didn't know what to do.

I finally came to understand that Jesus was asking me to focus my obsessive personality into being obsessed with him. I now understand that humans are born with an insatiable desire to become obsessed with just about anything. It could be relationships, material things, ideas, intellectual pursuits, money, etc. I believe, now, that I am a created being meant to be in contact with its creator.

It's normal to want to become obsessed with things—God put that into me. Although, it's important for me to be very careful not to put any other idol above Jesus Christ. I have learned to take my natural born instinct to become obsessed with things and indulge in Jesus Christ.

I have had a pattern of going from euphoria to despair because of chasing false idols. I was in desperate pain looking for a solution. I found the idols kept hurting me in the end.

I have found that Jesus is the *only* person who will *always* be there for me and *never* let me down. I can't say this about anyone else in my life. Over time and with experience, I have found Jesus to be reliable—I've had to build a relationship with Jesus, and that takes time.

I find that most things I love have limitations built into them, but Jesus has no limitations. I will always be growing and learning with Jesus. The relationship gets better and better over time as I invest in it—all of the other relationships in my life cannot possibly meet all my needs.

I find myself getting my significance from Jesus and nothing else. My purpose in life is to find my significance in a relationship with my creator. Now I can have fun with all these things I want to do, but I don't make the mistake of trying to find meaning and purpose in those pursuits. I am much happier now.

CHAPTER 16

Meant for Eternity

I am stuck in a world dictated to me by three things: my limitations, time, and the material. I believe, if most people are honest, they would admit that a bit of luck is involved in success. A person can do everything right and still fail. I believe the stars must align for a person to get what they want—it's why so many cultures around the world believe in fate or destiny.

I don't believe in the idea of a "self-made" man. Everyone got help outside their own efforts to become successful. Hard work is a large part of success, but it certainly isn't the whole story.

I realized, early on, that I am a slave to my limitations. I am stuck in a world where most of life is dictated to me. I have power somewhere in the mix, but I can't deny that there are much larger forces I am depending on to survive. My life could be taken from me at any moment.

I decided to take the chance that there is a power outside myself that I could tap into for help. My only hope to escape my huge limitations was to rely on something outside of the constraints of time and the material. I noticed that I am only as big as whatever I put my trust in. My only hope was in a miracle, so I decided to trust in Jesus Christ. After much research and deep thought, I decided to go the spiritual route.

I found the spiritual route to have the same value as the scientific route—both are necessary and important; however, I would be limited by the constraints of science if I chose only science. I see science as limited in explaining the larger invisible world around me. Science is only one part of the bigger picture. I conceded to the truth that science is far too limited in explaining the greater world—besides, science is a process, not a belief system.

I find relationships to be outside the realm of science; I find relationships to be a much better pursuit when trying to improve my life. Science is ok, but relationships are the key to happiness. Spirituality deals with relationship.

I chose to believe in God because I couldn't find a reason not to believe. I have done exhaustive research and found that it is rational to believe in God. I needed a force outside the constraints of time and material for help; I was a prisoner of time and material until I surrendered to the timeless and immaterial creator.

God is on the outside of our limited world looking in. He is the culmination of everything that is good. Rust and death hold no power over the creator that sent his son to show us he exists. We are in a temporary state here on Earth until the veil of death is lifted and eternity is made known; an eternity of union with each other and joy beyond belief. Ecclesiastes 3:11 says, "...He has also set eternity in the human heart..." My heart aches for something more because I am meant to live forever in paradise; I could never be satisfied in this world because I was made for eternity in heaven.

I don't believe that when I die I will become a god in the afterlife, like many believe. I am a created being that will be reunited with my creator when I die. Because we are created beings and not gods, we will continue to explore and discover, forever, the infinite universe after we die. The great adventure begins when believers pass through the door of death to continued growth in eternity. Jesus healed people and rescued them from death to show us how much he wants us to live in complete joy for eternity with him. For believers, death is the beginning of the greatest adventure of our lives.

CHAPTER 17

Jesus Won Me Over

I find that I am primarily driven by my emotions—I have found this to be true about everyone; not everyone will admit this is true because it's a terrifying thought. If you don't believe that people are primarily driven by emotion, just take a moment to look around the world.

The world is a madhouse. Go follow the news for any length of time, and you will see a world that is blindly chasing their desires with no thought of their fellow man. The weak are being stepped on while the strong justify their every move with religious fervor. I find selfish ambition at the heart of it all.

Where do I find the root of the problems in this world? I find the root of the problems locally. Look no further than the painful dramas being played out in our families. People should stop blaming politicians and start taking responsibility for their broken relationships with their family.

The politicians are there because people voted them in—the politicians are a reflection of the people they represent. People with families voted these politicians in place. The world's problems start with clearing up relationships in our families and neighborhoods. Better politicians will be chosen as people take responsibility for themselves. The best way to take responsibility for yourself is to submit to Jesus and be saved. You want to change the world? Look in the mirror.

I found myself breaking free of the madness as I challenged my own birth family. I lovingly confronted the relationships that were closest to me. I started to make boundaries for myself and apologized when I hurt someone selfishly. I decided to take responsibility for myself. I stopped making other people's problems my problem. I was willing to go through my own humiliation to find sanity by admitting my own limitations. When I was a part of the problem, I would take responsibility for myself.

Taking responsibility for myself set off seismic forces in my family. I got blamed for being a troublemaker because they wanted me to stop talking about the child abuse. I believe my siblings wanted me to go back to looking the other way because they were scared. I hated making the people I loved uncomfortable, but I could see no other way. My siblings were fellow victims of abuse as well, so there was no way to approach the topic of abuse without creating some chaos. It is a very painful topic for all of us—it is all very sad.

I found the old saying "you can't corner a square man" to be true. When everything looked bleak and hopeless, I would remind myself of the truth that I witnessed. I found that I didn't need anyone's permission to hold my own beliefs. I stopped looking for affirmation and validation in others; I started to believe what Jesus said about me. Jesus says that I am valuable and I matter. Jesus gave me the courage to move forward when it seemed that everyone was against me. Romans 8:31 says, "What, then, shall we say in response to these things? If God is for us, who can be against us?" I am a child of God; I am going to live forever—I should never obey fear.

I found refuge in Philippians 4:13 which says: "I can do all this through him who gives me strength." The verse is not saying I can do whatever I want and Christ will support me—the verse is telling me to bring my hurts to Jesus and he will tell me how to respond. This ensures that I am not acting out of selfish ambition—Jesus will help me to act in a loving way. I am submitting myself to Jesus and his solutions. I have found, over time, that Jesus is always the better way. I have learned to trust Jesus after bringing my hurts to him time and time again. I found myself apologizing more when I took matters into my own hands. As I trusted in Jesus, he won me over.

CHAPTER 18

PEACE

The moment I accepted Jesus Christ as my Lord and Savior, I found peace for the first time. I was in a place of total surrender, no longer striving to justify myself. I surrendered to the reality that I am a mortal man—I am limited and in need of my creator. I had found peace in the midst of hopelessness, helplessness, and unhappiness. Peace began to sooth my unhappiness and hurts; I found that my pain runs deep, but peace runs deeper.

All of my attempts at validating myself through personal accomplishments stopped. I no longer felt the need to carve out a place for myself in the world because I felt peaceful. Striving for anything seemed painful, hopeless, and unnecessary. I had the belief that nothing good could be accomplished without enduring pain. I believed in the "no pain, no gain" philosophy. I believed that meaning and purpose had to be generated by my own efforts.

After surrendering myself to God, my motivation shifted. I no longer had to prove myself. I found myself having achieved value simply through surrender. My new motivation came through my desire to be a part of the solution in the world. I no longer felt the master of selfish ambition driving me into situations that were over my head.

My desire to find ways to be a help in the world led me to looking into myself for attributes that came naturally and easily to me. I self-reflected and rested while I examined my life for things that brought joy to the world. In the beginning, it was difficult because I did not highly value my special character traits. I found that I enjoy making people feel good; I enjoy encouraging others. The world around me saw this character trait as useless and weak. It took courage for me to focus on my strengths rather than what the world around me was telling me. I had to trust that God could do something with this, seemingly, insignificant gift.

In the past, I resented my desire to make others feel good because it would get me hurt. I had a compulsion toward making people feel good at my own expense. I despised my desire to make others feel good because it was compulsive, and I got ran over by mean people easily. I had no way of protecting myself except to harden my personality. I would shame myself for being weak and admire people that seemed to have no conscience. I admired movie characters that weren't bothered by the compulsive drive to get along with others.

I admired stoicism. A stoic is a person who can endure pain or hardship without showing their feelings or complaining. I admired stoic characters that decided who they were going to help and who they would ignore. The stoic is not ruled by his emotions—that felt like a superpower to me.

Stoicism was failing me. I found stoicism alienating me from meaningful relationships. I was safe from being hurt, but I was also alienated from receiving love from others. I had successfully alienated any possibility of finding personal connection with my fellow human beings.

Jesus has shown me a better way. Jesus taught me how to be kind but firm. Jesus taught me to express my feelings, while at the same time, hold mean people accountable. I am free to express my hurts; I am free to cry.

Being hurt by someone says nothing negative about my character. For years I didn't allow myself to cry because I saw it as weakness. Crying can be a form of mourning and healing, if in the right context.

There is a difference between grief and mourning: Grief is the feeling I have when I am hurt; mourning is doing something intentionally to release that hurt. Grief is pain. Mourning is constructively and intentionally expressing that pain. I feel grief when someone says something mean to me; allowing myself to cry is mourning.

I believe it takes more strength to mourn than it does to hide grief. Hiding grief leaves the pain inside of you to never be released. Hiding grief leads to health problems and sadness. Hiding grief makes one lonely and disconnected from the relationships around them.

I now have no problem expressing my grief. I cry out when my feelings are hurt. I listen to my feelings, which helps me to be sensitive to what's happening around me. Ignoring grief blindfolds a person and makes them vulnerable to their emotions being manipulated by mean people. Our feelings are telling us when a person might be dangerous—or at the very least, harmful to us. Our feelings help us to discern situations if we don't ignore them.

I have learned to allow myself to feel deeply. Feeling deeply has raised my emotional quotient. Emotional quotient (EQ) determines a person's emotional intelligence. Emotional intelligence is decided by how well one can read people and social situations. If you want to raise your EQ, learn to have a conversation with your feelings.

If someone is mean to me, then I will cry. The whole time I am crying, I will be creating boundaries with the offender so I will not be hurt again. I will tell the offender that they must apologize to have the privilege of my company in the future. I create a boundary by giving the offender a hurdle they must jump through to continue in relationship with me. I will not tolerate bullying of any kind. Crying is not weakness—crying is healthy; although, not sticking up for yourself is weakness. Crying is how I mourn being hurt; crying is good for my health. I am a human being that feels—it is good to feel. I should cry and allow myself to hurt, but equally, I should be moving to create boundaries so I don't get hurt again. I should hold people accountable because I am honoring myself when I do so.

As a stoic, I was unable to detect a bully because my feelings were numb. Now my feelings are safe and free to be expressed because I have made boundaries with mean people. I found myself in the company of mean people quite often when I was emotionally clueless as a stoic. I am happier now because I don't spend any time with mean people—now, I deal with mean people decisively. I escort mean people out the door of my life the moment I find them. I will call the police if necessary. In an extreme situation, I will use deadly force in self-defense if they try to physically harm me or my family.

The Bible tells us to "stand" when we encounter evil. Ephesians 6:13 says, "Therefore put on the whole armor of God, so that when the day of evil comes, you may be able to stand your ground, and after you have done everything, to stand." We are not supposed to provoke bullies. We are also not supposed to run from bullies. The Bible says to "stand your ground." Cowards run, bullies attack, and brave people stand their ground. It is loving to stand your ground.

I will be kind to the bully, but I will also be firm. I don't want to allow the bully to make me ugly like them. I do what Jesus told me to do. I will love the bully by not tolerating their cruel behavior, while at the same time, giving them instructions on how to get back into relationship with me. I always give a person that I have rejected a way back to me, but it must be on my terms—that is how to love a bully; that is how to express my feelings while dealing decisively with mean people. In Matthew 10:16, Jesus said, "I am sending you out like sheep among wolves. Therefore be as shrewd as snakes and as innocent as doves."

CHAPTER 19

METAPHOR

Perhaps the greatest influence on me was when I read *The Hobbit* and *The Lord of the Rings* trilogy back in 1985. I was in sixth grade. I invited these stories into my life because I felt no sense of being manipulated by someone. The stories came as sweet-smelling, buttered popcorn or freshly baked bread. I was a defensive and hardened boy at the time. I believe Jesus used *The Lord of The Rings* trilogy to reach me when nothing else could. I had no idea that I opened myself to a message of hope when I opened those books.

The trilogy gently called to me, then wrapped me in a warm embrace. I felt myself identifying with the struggle Frodo had with the ring; the relationship Frodo had with the ring paralleled my life. I had been living in overwhelming darkness—the darkness saturated me and threatened to destroy me.

The Lord of the Rings works as a metaphor. The story paralleled the struggle between good and evil inside my heart. The genre of *The Lord of The Rings* is fantasy. The writer, JRR Tolkien, delivers a very real struggle that was happening in my heart. Much like the evil ring of power, I felt the draw of evil telling me to drown my misery in selfish pursuits. Evil was driving me to self-destruct.

Ralph Waldo Emerson famously said, "Fiction reveals truth that reality obscures."

After going through much pain and fear, the desire to medicate my pain was more than I could bear. I found myself running into destructive behaviors with little regard for my own safety. I was running toward alcohol to escape the pain I was in from the abuse I suffered.

In my world, the evil ring represented my constant efforts to overwhelm my pain with feeling good. I was pursuing selfish ambition and medicating my hurts to avoid looking at myself with a sober mind. I hated who I was, so I was constantly striving to find wonderful distractions. Distractions that kept me from seeing the reality that I was desperately limited in a dangerous world.

The main character, Frodo, was on a mission to destroy the ring. The ring called to Frodo, compelling him to take matters into his own hands. Frodo was in a struggle to salvage his humanity. When Frodo gave into the ring, he found himself being mean to the people around him and seeking his own glory at the expense of others.

I, too, saw that evil was trying to steal my ability to empathize with myself and others around me. I found myself justifying my self-destructive behaviors. I would justify my self-destructive behaviors by adopting a belief system that there is no good in the world—I struggled between hope and hopelessness.

More and more I found myself letting go of the idea that hope is real. Evil seemed much stronger than good, so I found myself looking for ways to indulge in self-destructive tendencies without causing too much damage. I would lean into evil and hopelessness from time to time, just to numb myself from the reality that my life was meaningless and hopeless.

Hope was always calling me in the opposite direction—hope seemed so small. I would ask myself, "Why should I keep suffering this humiliating dance between light and darkness?!" I felt as if hope were making a fool of me. Hope can be very painful. I wanted to give up many times, but I would keep finding things to carry me forward. *The Lord of the Rings* carried me forward; it is a great metaphor for my life struggles.

I did not understand the effect the book had on me at the time—that is what made it so wonderful. A message of hope was delivered to me through a story and not by a judgmental person. God used a wonderful story to speak to me. I did not trust people, yet God had delivered a message of hope to me safely. I didn't understand the powerful hope the book had given me until many years later. I was inspired by seeing Frodo struggle through pain to make the world a better place.

The story empathized with me; it spoke into my own feelings of dread and hope. The story is a metaphor for the human condition and the fight between good and evil in our own lives. I found out, many years later, that JRR Tolkien was a devout Christian. Tolkien had thoughtfully and gently sewn his Christianity into a story—a seemingly harmless story. Jesus spoke to me in a "still, small voice" through Tolkien's prose. The Christian message had been delivered to me in a nonthreatening way. The story of *The Lord of the Rings* called me forward into hope, unbeknownst to me. The harmless story was perfect in its delivery of the message of hope.

CHAPTER 20

A Still, Small Voice

I have found that Jesus is gentle, kind, and unobtrusive. Jesus is very careful with his injured children. I have learned to ignore voices that don't consider my feelings, and my feelings are very important to Jesus Christ.

God spoke to his prophet Elijah in a "still, small voice." 1 Kings 19:11–12 says:

Then the Lord said, 'Go out and stand on the mountain before the Lord. Behold, the Lord is about to pass by.' And a great and mighty wind tore into the mountains and shattered the rocks before the Lord, but the Lord was not in the wind. After the wind there was an earthquake, but the Lord was not in the earthquake. After the earthquake there was a fire, but the Lord was not in the fire. And after the fire came a still, small voice.

The Berean Study Bible translates this as saying, "a still, small voice." Other translations say, "the sound of a low whisper" or "a gentle whisper" or "a soft whisper" or "the sound of a gentle blowing."

To find God's voice, I have learned to quiet my soul and meditate on peaceful thoughts. Jesus is the most gentle person I have ever heard speak. Jesus understands what I have been through; Jesus respects my pain.

Isaiah 42:3 says, "A bruised reed he will not break, and a smoldering wick he will not snuff out. In faithfulness he will bring forth justice." Jesus is gentle with the broken hearted and wounded—Jesus protects; Jesus understands.

In Matthew 11:28-30, Jesus says, "Come to me, all who are weary and burdened, and I will give you rest. Take my yoke upon you and learn from me: for I am gentle and humble in heart, and you will find rest for your souls. For my yoke is easy and my burden is light." I understand how to discern God's voice in the world with so many distractions. God's voice is behind all of the noise—God's voice is gentle and sweet. I am inspired by how Jesus addresses me. I encourage you not to give up and to listen for his voice.

In John 10:27-28, Jesus said, "My sheep hear my voice, and I know them, and they follow me: And I give unto them eternal life; and they shall never perish, neither shall any man pluck them out of my hand." Jesus loves me more than anyone I have ever met. Jesus is my advocate.

There are many counterfeit voices trying to charm me with lies. I have learned that Jesus wants me to go slow, and he is never in a hurry. I have learned patience and discernment. Jesus is helping me learn how to love myself through loving him first.

My assignment is not easy but it is simple. The Bible says in Matthew 6:33: "Seek first his kingdom and his righteousness, and all these things will be given as well." I find that Jesus wants to guide me and protect me; Jesus wants me to grow.

Jesus asks for me to be intentional about everything I do. Jesus wants me to bring everything to him first before I act. Jesus helps me grow in wisdom and understanding as I allow him to go before me throughout this world. I find life makes more sense and it has meaning as I surrender to God's ways. My belief in God grows as I see him working in my life; I seek God first and surrender my ambitions to him. When I do understand the task in front of me, I am free to pursue it with ambition. Jesus only asks that I always check in with him first. I find my life gaining meaning and purpose as I seek him first in all things.

CHAPTER 21

INTIMACY

It was when I was walking to school one morning that I first saw pornography. There was a colorful magazine page lying on the ground; I reached down, picked it up, and saw the most beautiful thing I had ever seen in my life.

The most wonderful, euphoric feeling came over my body as I gazed at the beautiful naked girl. I felt so deeply flattered that this girl would show me her most intimate side. I fell in love—it was love at first sight, for sure. I lived in a world of loneliness and rejection, and this made me feel wonderful.

I knew right away that it was wrong—a moment later I balled up the paper and threw it down, although it was too late. All the crushing pain I was in had subsided, if only for a brief moment.

As soon as school was out, like a starving person, I hurried back to where I had thrown down the angel. She was gone; I couldn't find her. It made me feel even more sad and alone—I needed her.

For her to show me this intimate side of herself—it made me feel accepted, connected, complete, and safe. Like a loving, accepting mother, she cradled me in her arms and made everything right in my life, if only for a moment. My undernourished, empty heart was starving for intimacy. I was hopelessly smitten.

Everyone has emotional needs. There are healthy ways to meet those emotional needs and unhealthy ways. Pornography and sex addiction are unhealthy ways to meet those needs.

Sex is more than physical feelings—there are emotional needs trying to be met, as well. The emotional part of sex is what makes it dangerous to our mental health. Through sex, people are unwittingly trying to meet their emotional needs. Sex is a vulnerable act. When people have sex, they are leaving themselves open to being hurt at a deep level.

Being naked in font of another individual opens you up to being judged, which can hurt you very badly. When we are naked, we are exposing many of our flaws. All people have an overwhelming desire to be accepted. Sex can be very flattering. People become addicted to the feeling of being loved unconditionally. Our hearts naturally seek unconditional love because God made us to be in union with him. Many people find counterfeit ways to recreate feelings of love, and sex outside of marriage promises that it will cure your feelings of loneliness and of inferiority. Sex outside of marriage is euphoric at first, but then it leaves you feeling worse than before—it leaves you feeling empty and more vulnerable because you have just handed your personal security to someone else. You have given your heart to someone you have not made a commitment toward.

In the beginning, in the Garden of Eden, humans were naked. People were naked and felt no need to wear clothes because there was no sin in the world. People had perfect union with their creator—there was no reason to fear attack or ridicule. The world was perfect.

When sin entered the world, Adam and Eve began to cover themselves up for the first time. Adam and Eve used fig leaves to cover their naked bodies. They covered their bodies because, now, they could tell they were vulnerable—evil had entered the relationship. Now that their mate had the option to be evil, they could use that evil to hurt them. Covering the body is how they were trying to protect themselves from being hurt.

Nudist colonies are a good example of people trying to recreate the time before sin entered the world. Nudist colonies are trying, in vain, to recreate the situation in the Garden of Eden. Man has been trying to fill the gap between themselves and God with all sorts of damaging pursuits.

It is euphoric to be accepted flaws and all. Being rejected is devastating. Sex is a risky venture. After both sexual partners have had sex, an extreme paranoia can set in. People have a tendency to be cruel when they are trying to protect themselves from ridicule. The relationship goes from wonderful to terrifying overnight. Our need for love and acceptance drives us down a destructive path—the more promiscuous sex a person has, the more they damage their conscience.

Seeking sex and intimacy is how people unknowingly try and recreate the Garden of Eden. People are trying to experience paradise when they seek fulfillment in sex outside of marriage. Before mankind rebelled against God, we lived in paradise. Our hearts crave paradise and union with God; therefore, sex is how people try to recapture that feeling. Sex is a gift from God.

We are meant to be in perfect union with our creator. Our hearts crave intimacy; our hearts crave closeness and friendship. Our brains perform mental gymnastics in their efforts to justify risky sex. People are in pain, so they seek a quick fix in sex outside of marriage.

Most people underestimate their need for meaningful relationship, and sex is treated flippantly. The movies and TV programs only show half the picture. Sex outside of marriage always comes at a heavy price; there is no avoiding it.

Intimacy is what everyone wants, whether you are heterosexual, homosexual, transgendered, etc. Intimacy is what our hearts crave. People are lonely so they crave intimacy. Heterosexuality doesn't get you into heaven, just like homosexuality doesn't keep you out—it doesn't matter what your sexual preference is. God wants a contrite heart. An unrepentant heterosexual will go to hell; a repentant homosexual will go to heaven. What keeps a person out of heaven is their pride, not sexual preferences. Proverbs 16:18 says, "Pride goes before destruction, and haughty spirit before a fall." We will have evil desires before and after we are saved, but a surrendered heart will turn ashes into diamonds.

Sex inside of marriage can also be complicated, but there has been a commitment that is not easily broken. There is more safety in marriage than sex outside of marriage. Hurts will happen, but the promise made under oath to each other and the legal obligations protect each other from being abandoned easily—there is protection. Marriage is a binding promise to protect the husband and wife from bailing prematurely on the relationship.

God puts another person in our lives by marriage to help us become better people. If we have a Christ-centered marriage, then we will find personal growth. I have found, as I fight for my marriage, I grow in wisdom about myself and the world. I become more empathetic—that empathy allows me to better navigate all the relationships in the world. I learn to appreciate that we are emotional beings that want to feel safe. As I create a safe place in my marriage, I become a safer person to others. People flourish in safety; relationships prosper when there is safety.

As I try to understand my spouse more, I become more sensitive to the needs of people around me. I become less self-centered. I become a better human being when I surrender my marriage to God and humble myself to be corrected.

I also learn to be more assertive if I have been passive or weak. God uses our spouse to help us understand his character. My spouse is there to help me become a better person. Most people become discouraged when there are problems in their marriage, but the problems are a part of God's plan. Marriage problems are normal.

I found that intimacy is a need that I must learn how to meet for myself. I find that everyone is a sexual being. Experiencing sexual intimacy works much like fire: fire can be very destructive, but fire can also be a source of warmth and safety. If a fire gets started in the woods with no containment, it will rage out of control and destroy lives, but if I put the fire in a fireplace, then it is safely manageable and life-giving.

Sex is the same as fire—when it is handled with care and responsibility, it is life-giving. God gave mankind marriage as a way of managing lust. Marriage is the fireplace for sex so it doesn't burn out of control; marriage is the safe place that intimacy can fully be expressed.

I have found lust to be impossible to overcome on one's own. I believe this is normal. God put sexual desire into both men and women—it is normal and healthy to desire people sexually. The strength of lust can only be managed. Marriage is the best way to manage sexual desire. Sexual desire will never be overcome in this lifetime. Marriage is the best coping mechanism that God has given us to keep sex healthy.

Jesus talks about lust in Matthew 5:27-30. Jesus said:

You have heard that it was said, 'Do not commit adultery.' But I tell you anyone who looks at a woman to lust after her has already committed adultery with her in his heart. If your right eye causes you to sin, gouge it out and throw it away. It is better for you to lose one part of your body than for your whole body to be thrown into hell. And if your right hand causes you to sin, cut it off and throw it away. It is better for you to lose one part of your body than for your whole body to depart into hell.

Jesus is showing, in this verse, that he doesn't tolerate any form of sexual sin. It is true that God does not tolerate sin—God takes sin very seriously.

So, why does Jesus talk about "gouging out eyes" and "cutting off hands"? That is a terrifying thing to say. Does God actually expect us to gouge out our eyes and cut off our hand if we lust? If we are fallen beings and we can't escape sin, isn't that a cruel thing to say to people that can't help it? After all, we were all born into a sinful world and it's inevitable we will lust. Isn't that cruel? Is Jesus being a meanie here?

I believe Jesus mentions lust and violently maiming ourselves in the same breath to destroy any sense of hope we might have in our own strength. Jesus wants us to despair, get overwhelmed, and fall helplessly into his arms. Jesus is overwhelming us with the idea of overcoming lust by our own strength. By telling us something as ridiculous as to maim ourselves, he is showing how it is equally ridiculous to try and overcome lust on our own.

I believe that many well-meaning Christians are stuck in a cycle of legalism and shame, never knowing God's grace, because they want to overcome lust on their own. They have taken Christ out of the picture, in their arrogance and zeal, to prove they are worthy. The Bible says that none of us are worthy.

Romans 3:10-20 says:

As it is written: There is no one righteous, not even one. There is no one who understands, no one who seeks God. All have turned away, they have together become worthless; there is no one who does good, not even one. Their throats are open graves; their tongues practice deceit. The venom of vipers is on their lips. Their mouths are full of cursing and bitterness. Their feet are swift to shed blood; ruin and misery lie in their wake, and the way of peace they have not known. There is no fear of God before their eyes. Now we know that whatever the law says, it says to those that are under the law, so that every mouth may be silenced and the whole world held accountable to God. Therefore no one will be justified in his sight by works of the law. For the works of law merely brings awareness of sin.

I believe God is talking about believers and nonbelievers here. If you are honest with yourself, then you will see that you are capable of hurting others. I practice apologizing to others because it is inevitable that I will hurt someone's feelings. I am a fickle soul, capable of being both helpful and hurtful.

2 Corinthians 3:6 says: "He has made us competent as ministers of a new covenant—not of the letter but of the spirit; for the letter kills but the spirit gives life." The "letter" mentioned here is referring to man's effort to keep the laws of God rather than surrender to God's care. The spirit is Jesus. Trying to follow God by our own power leads to despair; surrendering to the spirit is our only hope.

Christians and non-Christians have in common the fact that we are all guilty of sin and selfish ambition. The only thing that sets us apart is grace, not our works. We should be humble and not think ourselves better than the unbeliever. These verses are pointing out that we are capable of much the same destruction that nonbelievers are. We should live life surrendered and on our knees at all times; we should always live the same as the moment we first surrendered our lives to Jesus and in every moment thereafter. We never reach a place where we can do life on our own power.

Lust is one of the ways that God reminds us that we cannot do life on our own. Lust reminds us that we are dependent on God. We will never overcome lust. I believe lust can be out of control and brought into submission by God; however, we never will defeat lust completely in this lifetime.

Lust happens so fast that we can't help it. I believe we can't stop ourselves from lusting; lust is inevitable. Jesus said that we are guilty of adultery in our heart if we look at someone with lust—Jesus understands this and he has a kind response to us.

I have found that both women and men are equally capable of lust. These verses are for both men and women. What I am saying is that we cannot overcome lust by our own power—we need Jesus to help us.

The apostle Paul in 2 Corinthians 12:7-10 spoke of a "thorn in the flesh" he was given by God to keep him humble.

...So to keep me from becoming conceited, I was given a thorn in my flesh, a messenger of Satan, to torment me. Three times I pleaded with the Lord to take it away from me. But he said to me, 'My grace is sufficient for you, for my power is perfected in weakness.' Therefore I will boast all the more gladly in my weaknesses, so that the power of Christ may rest on me. That is why, for the sake of Christ, I delight in weaknesses, in persecutions, in difficulties. For when I am weak, then I am strong.

Did Paul ever lust? I believe he did. Could this struggle Paul had be lust? Maybe. No one knows what Paul's thorn was. I believe it could have just as easily been lust. We are to deal with lust in the same way Paul dealt with his thorn—we surrender and fall into Jesus Christ's arms and let him deliver us from lust.

We are to live life on our knees. We let our failures remind us that we are wretches, saved by Jesus from death. We should live life cautiously. We should be happy and full of hope, yet humble. We remind ourselves that we are children of God, but we are not free of this world until we die. We should be happy and live a life surrendered in joy to our creator who takes care of us. We should enjoy all God's goodness but never forget where we came from.

Lust lost when Jesus died on the cross and was raised from the dead—it no longer has a grip on our lives. We are winners in the winner's circle. Let Jesus do the hard work and let us have fun bringing his love and joy to the world. We are no longer under the burden of trying to be perfect. We are imperfect and beautiful children of God, destined for eternal happiness. I will smile and embrace each day, believing that my destination is heaven.

I will sin from time to time, but I should be quick to repent—what a joy that I am no longer tethered by death! Even my habitual sins do not separate me from God. I am to remain surrendered and trust that God will continue to do good work in me, despite my sin. What a joy!

In time, I learned how to better manage my need for intimacy. As I surrendered to Jesus and let him guide me, it brought me to seek help with others who were struggling with similar problems. It required humility and courage. I sought help from the church leaders—those leaders were not perfect and they did let me down in many ways over time.

As I remained committed to Jesus and not men, Jesus used imperfect people to help me. Eventually, many of those leaders let me down for some reason or another, but I remained honest with myself. I never threw out my journey toward healing because of a few jerks along the way. God even used the jerks at some level; I was grateful for any help I could get. The leaders let me down but Christ never let me down.

I found that healing is much like eating a fish with bones in it: the bad advice and selfish cruelty that I met along the way were the bones in the fish; the meat of the fish was the nutrients I gathered from my commitment to God. I simply learned to eat around the bones.

I never let bitterness steal my victory. I used forgiveness often in order to discern between the good advice and the selfish motivations of mean people. A forgiving heart keeps me tuned into hearing God's voice.

Through forgiveness, Jesus kept me on his path to healing. I would quit people that became toxic, yet, I never quit Jesus—this is how I protected myself from becoming controlled by the selfish motivations of people.

Forgiveness is how God protected me from the evil motivations of men. Forgiveness opened my eyes to corruption and helped me to see who Jesus was in clarity. Forgiving others taught me how to discern people. In the beginning, reaching out for help was terrifying in a world where I saw most people as selfishly motivated and not interested in me. I was clueless on how to build healthy relationships and it was terrifying to rely on others. Forgiveness kept me soft, pliable, and teachable.

In the beginning, I was hurt by selfish leaders. In time, I learned to discern between people that were genuine and people that only wanted to use me. As I look back, I see God using all the people in my life to reach me, no matter their intentions. I ran from mean people, and I never allowed myself to grow so hard-hearted that I couldn't be reached by genuine people.

I was a clueless kid. It was a scary walk, but I never gave up on Jesus; people let me down, but Jesus was always there. In time, I learned that I should never put my full trust in anyone except Jesus. I learned that Jesus is the *only* person who would *always* be there for me and *never* let me down. As a young naive kid, I put too much trust in people—in time, I learned how to protect myself.

CHAPTER 22

THE GOOD NEWS

No matter how bad things get in my life, I can always reflect on the fact that my life is sustained by good news. The first four books of the New Testament contain the teachings of Jesus Christ. The first four books are referred to as the gospel. The "gospel" simply means "good news."

The good news is that I have become a child of the King of Kings—I have been adopted into the royal lineage of God. Before, I was a limited person with no special talents to speak of; my future prospects were bad.

I was an abused child that thought of myself as garbage. I was told I was garbage by my father, and my mother wanted nothing to do with me. All of this was reinforced by violent, systematic beatings from the ages of four to nine years old. My parents moved us to another state when I was ten, and the chaos from the move stopped the systematic beatings from my dad.

The good news was that during all of these devastating times, God had adopted me to be his own. I started believing in Jesus when I was a child. For a time, I was excited about God. In time, though, the nightmare I had entered overwhelmed my moment with Jesus. My life was in turmoil.

Looking back, I can see that a little flame had been kindled inside of me at a young age—that fire was pure and good and would not tolerate any sort of evil. As a result, my heart began to rage against the way I was treated. I had tasted hope, and once I got that taste, I began a mission to find the source of the evil. I fell into a deep, righteous anger toward evil, and I began to despise evil and love what is good.

The good news is that Jesus has given me a taste of freedom. I suddenly felt free because Jesus showed me that there is an alternative way to view my circumstances. I was a prisoner of darkness—all I knew was fear. I was tiny and helpless. But Jesus split the darkness for a moment and revealed himself to me; I saw another way. Jesus is all that is good; Jesus is pure love and light.

I was a slave to fear until Jesus revealed himself to me. Jesus adopted me into his family. I had tasted true love and my heart raged against the darkness to taste of love again.

The moment I was saved, I felt freedom for the first time. Freedom of fear; freedom of tyranny. My heart had felt freedom, and I wasn't going to settle for anything less.

My beatings increased and became systematic after I was saved. I became unruly and impossible to control—I was no longer downcast in my face. I became hopeful, loving, and persevering in trials.

I was a savage that tasted the goodness of God's table. My heart raged against the darkness and evil. I began to fight and endure with a new ferocity. I became a warrior for light in a world full of darkness. My earthly father was a slave to fear, and a slave of fear will severely punish anyone who dares to upset his ruthless master. My father was dominated by fear; my father was a slave of darkness.

The good news came in the form of tasting freedom—Jesus told me that I am no longer subject to the rulers and authorities of this world. In John 16:33, Jesus says, "I have told you these things so that in me you may have peace. In the world you will have tribulation. But take courage; I have overcome the world!"

I didn't have the intellectual understanding of what had taken place when I was saved because I was a child. I later found the words to describe what happened to me. In its most basic form, Jesus had planted an unquenchable fire within me—he had planted hope. That hope burned as an eternal flame; that hope brought me a new terrible pain. The pain of hope—hope raged against hopelessness.

With Jesus in my heart, I am compelled to bring his love and justice into the world. I feel hatred for evil. I will not tolerate evil anymore—I will work against the evil in my heart and the evil in the world. The good news is that Jesus has claimed me as his own, and therefore, I will not tolerate any form of tyranny or injustice. I will confront evil on every front. I have become dangerous to bullies; I have become a thorn in the side of those who would do evil.

This world is a stepping stone into the next. My suffering here on Earth is short compared to eternity in paradise. I keep my eyes fixed on Jesus and trust him. Jesus has saved me from being a slave to fear—I owe Jesus my life. I serve Jesus out of a deep well of love. He rescued me from the darkness. I will be afraid at times, but never a slave to fear again. Jesus has shown me that love is stronger than fear. I was raised in fear, but Jesus snatched me out of the jaws of fear. I am no longer afraid of death; I am a child of God. My father was fear—now, my Father is love.

My life has been a steady growth from darkness to light. I am growing in my ability to trust Jesus. As I grow older and my body fails, I find myself building momentum in hope. That small flame in me is growing into a holy, raging fire—a raging fire of love that evil flees from in terror. The good news is that death and fear lost when I surrendered to Jesus and began to trust him. The good news is that I have been bought by the blood of Christ. I find my identity in Jesus Christ. Psalm 118:6: "The Lord is with me; I will not be afraid. What can mere mortals do to me?"

CHAPTER 23

Sanctification

My relationship has been growing with God over the years as I have trusted in him. Early in my relationship with Jesus Christ, I had more of the world's values—I believed that I had to build my worth through self-discipline. The two hurdles I had to jump were my own weaknesses and a hostile world that wanted to see me fail. My self-worth was out there on the horizon to be won by my own will and determination—also, if I did win my self-worth, then I had to fight to keep it. My self-worth was as elusive as Bigfoot or aliens.

I had huge ambition and visions of grandeur—I was going to be somebody worth knowing. I wanted to be someone so strong that no one could hurt me ever again. I wanted to be ten feet tall and bullet proof—I valued physical strength above everything else.

In hindsight, I can see that these ambitions were my efforts to compensate for what my father and mother did to me. I was compensating for being violently beaten and bullied by my father. In time, Jesus showed me that I was merely reacting to what happened to me as a child without much thought; I was in a panic, trying to overcompensate for my weaknesses. My father had beat on me at a most tender age, and then said that I was garbage and would never amount to anything. The most important people in my life, my parents, had marked me for disposal. I was defective; a bad part that needed to be thrown out—this was all reinforced with violence.

I felt like Sisyphus in Greek mythology. Sisyphus was condemned for eternity to roll a rock up to the top of a mountain, only to have the rock roll back down to the bottom—he was condemned to roll a boulder uphill for eternity. I was trying to figure out a way to escape this curse. I threw myself at ridiculously high, ambitious projects to try and overcome the curse. I tried to be an NFL football player for a time; I did Golden Gloves boxing for a time. I only pursued physical goals because I was most afraid of being overpowered again—overpowered like my father had overpowered me.

I felt the need to win back my right to be a human being. I had lost my soul and I had to win it back. I felt that I didn't have the same rights as other people. I thought that I had lost my human rights. I was an outcast; subhuman; unworthy.

I would ambitiously pursue a goal and then burn out. I would meet many of the goals that I would pursue, but I still felt empty, unworthy, and unsatisfied. I would meet my smaller goals along the way, but I would only despair because of the emptiness I felt afterwards.

I came to understand, through trial and error, that my self-worth was won the moment I accepted Jesus Christ as my Lord and Savior—my value never comes into question when I live under God's word. I was hopelessly trying to fill a bottomless pit with my own efforts to become relevant. I had no joy because I was ambitiously pursuing something that can only be given to me by God. I was ambitiously pursuing my right to live and exist, when the very act of God creating me makes me a priceless work of art.

The hands of the creator molded me and brought me into the world. He decided I should live; he decided I am valuable. I gave up my vain pursuits and set my heart on learning God's ways. I decided to let God dictate what I should do. I surrendered by giving up my own ambitious projects. I embraced what God was telling me would give me life. With a great sigh of relief, I fell into Christ's arms and let him begin to lead me. I was exhausted and defeated so I humbled myself and began to trust God.

Sometimes, I would find myself being led astray by seemingly wonderful pursuits. After running aimlessly for a bit, I would surrender, which brought me back into line with God's will—this is a countless cycle that I went through, and happened more frequently in the beginning, but as I learned to discern between God's voice and Satan's lies, my life became more sane and peaceful. This process of messing up, then cleaning up is called sanctification; sanctification is the process of being freed from sin. I am being purified.

I would repent each time I sinned by surrendering myself to Jesus. I learned to let God give me direction as opposed to ambitiously pursuing what I thought would give me life. I traded my ways for God's ways. Isaiah 55:8-9 says, "'For my thoughts are not your thoughts, neither are your ways my ways,' declares the Lord. 'As the heavens are higher than the earth, so are my ways higher than your ways and my thoughts than your thoughts.'"

God led me out of a life of desperate, hopeless, pursuits and into a life of meaning and purpose. My value is no longer on trial—I am free to pursue whatever I want to with no need to justify myself. I have been made righteous by Jesus Christ; I have found peace in the midst of adversity and pain.

CHAPTER 24

Beyond a Reasonable Doubt

Let's assume for a minute that everything in the Bible is true. The Bible says we are being punished for our rebellion against God, yet God has given us a way back to him—our time here on Earth is a chance to reunite with our creator in paradise. We have free will. We can choose God or we can choose our own way, which leads to hell. The world makes the most sense to me when I recognize it is a place where people get to choose if they will follow God or not.

I have come to trust in God. I have found my belief in Jesus to be reliable. I haven't been able to disprove that God exists. It's been the opposite of what I imagined—I have found it much more likely that there is a God than not. I find overwhelming evidence there is a God.

I haven't found hard evidence for the belief in God, but I also haven't found any hard evidence that there isn't a God. Court cases are won when the evidence is beyond a reasonable doubt—I believe that belief in God easily meets the requirement of beyond a reasonable doubt. If beyond a reasonable doubt is good enough to put a criminal away for life in prison or to prevent an innocent person from going to prison…it's good enough for me to put my faith in. My belief in Jesus Christ meets all of the legal criteria. Dr. Sean McDowell is the expert I turn to when looking for evidence that Jesus is true.

I believe and trust in Jesus Christ; I believe Jesus Christ is true—this brings my life meaning and purpose. If the Bible is true, then that means that our time on Earth is only a very short stay—at best we get around one hundred years.

I am able to better endure because I am comparing one hundred years to eternity. One hundred years is the equivalent of the short doorstep into a home; this world is the doorstep into eternity. How long is one hundred years compared to eternity? I can't begin to calculate those numbers.

I have been alive for fifty plus years now—those years went by frighteningly fast. The remaining time I have will go faster than I want it to as well. I have used most of my time to investigate if Jesus is God. I find that I have used my time well because I have gained confidence that there is a God. Considering all the abuse I have unfairly received, it's been tremendously helpful.

I find that belief in God works the same as belief in an individual. It takes time to build trust in a relationship. Jesus Christ is a relationship—he is not a set of rules or principles to live by; he is a living being. He is the God man. He lived on Earth for about thirty years then returned to sit at the right hand of God the father.

Jesus mentioned paradise when he was hanging on the cross. In Luke 23:43, Jesus said to the thief hanging on the other cross next to him: "Truly I tell you, today you will be with me in paradise." Paradise?! Let's assume this is true for a minute. I have a difficult time trying to understand what paradise would look like, but I can imagine it's much better than my time on earth today. My reward for believing and trusting in Jesus Christ is paradise when my body dies.

I can choose to live, believing that when I die, everything stops, like turning off the television. I can live as if there is nothing when I die; I can live, believing there is no accountability for how I treat others.

My motivation for how I live is different depending on which view I decide to hold about life after death. When I believe my life ends in a moment and there is nothing else...I feel a sense of desperation and loneliness grip me. Fear becomes my chief enemy; time becomes a cruel master. I feel a sense of dread that I need to overwhelm with a sense of purpose. I become anxious, searching for anything I can, to rid myself of the feelings of impending doom. My life becomes dark and desperate.

I find myself losing empathy for human suffering because it's far too demanding and it reminds me of my own mortality. I run from anything that reminds me of death like a crazed animal, escaping a forest fire. I find myself living in a panic, trying to squeeze any bit of meaning I can out of a dying and brutal world.

On the contrary, I can live as if death is the beginning of my time in eternal paradise. Death is not the end. When I live as if I am going to live forever, I find that time is not against me; time is not my master. I live with hope and a sense of peace when knowing my destination.

If the Bible is true, then I will only suffer a little while. I remember to stop and smell the roses. I take longer to enjoy a beautiful sunset. I sit longer with my daughter, soaking up the love that she naturally emanates. I find relationships more valuable. I move at a slower pace. I have no room for panic or fear. I find myself nurturing love and valuing effort to clear up my relationships. I value people more than accomplishments. I work toward making the world a better place. I am open to experiencing happiness when it suddenly shows up. I experience happiness—happiness is no longer elusive. A deeper peace begins to take hold and sustain me no matter how terrible things may get.

I have lived both: a life without God and a life with God. I find meaning and purpose only when I live for God. Living as if there is no God always ends in despair and hopelessness—it's exhausting trying to generate meaning out of a meaningless existence.

I begin to transcend time as I live for Jesus Christ; I begin to live for eternity. Living for God removes me from the rat race. I transcend this world and become born again into eternity.

I feel compelled to make the world a better place, out of my gratefulness to Jesus Christ. Jesus Christ saved me from fear. I want to follow Jesus and bring peace; I want to be a part of the solution in this world; I want to free others from the bondage of fear; I want to use my time to encourage others around me, rather than pursuing selfish gain. My time in this world becomes meaningful, and I feel compelled to share this good news with others.

I feel a sense of responsibility to this world; I feel a responsibility to share the peace I have experienced. Jesus taught me empathy for others. I feel a responsibility to use money to serve people and *not* use people to serve money. Human life has become sacred, and selfish ambition has become toxic. I do what I can to make the world a better place because people are infinitely valuable and worthy.

I like who I am when I believe in God—I don't like who I am when I don't believe in God. My belief in God is the thermometer that tests my level of wellness.

CHAPTER 25

Safety

I have been married for twenty-five plus years now, and I have a daughter that's nine years old as this is being written. I have found that a safe environment is key to prosperity. I dedicate my home to Jesus Christ; I want to have a Christ-centered home environment, and I lead by example.

I do not expect anyone to do anything that I am not willing to do myself. I create an environment of love and respect—I do this by allowing everyone to hold each other accountable with Galatians 5:22-23, which says: "But the fruit of the spirit is love, joy, peace, patience, kindness, goodness, faithfulness, gentleness, and self-control. Against such things there is no law."

My wife created a beautiful hand-drawn picture of this verse that we placed in the center of our house for all to see. It is not a set of rules or principles—it is God's living word, inspiring us to remember him as we go throughout our day. It is more of a symbol than a sign. A sign points you in a direction, whereas a symbol itself is the object of attention. 2 Timothy 3:16-17 says, "All scripture is God-breathed and is useful for teaching, rebuking, correcting and training in righteousness, so that the servant of God may be thoroughly equipped for every good work."

Scripture is God's word—it is special. Scripture is alive if you have the correct perspective. When reflecting on Scripture with a contrite heart, it will speak to you; God will speak to you. It is not a set of directions but a spirit to be filled by. Let the Scripture fill you and change you. Scripture is a living power, unlike any normal document written by hand—one should be especially attentive and thoughtful when reading Scripture.

I lead my family by surrendering myself to the headship of Christ. I become a conduit for the Holy Spirit. I purify myself by confessing my sins to God. I take responsibility for myself first before expecting others to follow me. 1 Corinthians 11:1 says, "Follow my example as I follow the example of Christ."

I follow Christ first, then I trust that he will help my family to want to do the same. I cannot make anyone do anything without expecting resistance. I do not push my family; I try to become a sweet smell that they will want to follow. It's better to draw people like bees to honey than it is to drive them like cattle. I surrender myself to Christ and become the person that they would want to follow.

If people don't feel safe, then nothing will get done. I can pull my authority as father and force them to obey in the moment. I can use fear or intimidation—this works in the short term, yet no one will follow a person like that for long. I can make my child sit down and listen to me. The problem is that, metaphorically, my daughter would be sitting down on the outside but standing up on the inside. She would endure until she escaped me. Jesus doesn't force anyone to believe in him. If Jesus doesn't force people, then how much more useless if I try? I remove my ego from the equation through surrender to God.

I create an environment of safety for my family. I ask that no one raise their voice—there can be no criticism until there is safety; whatever is said should be said with gentleness and respect. If

I get impatient and raise my voice, then I should ask the family's forgiveness before anything else is said—otherwise, the conversation will go nowhere.

Creativity only prospers in an environment where there is no criticism. When I want to maximize my creativity, I will brainstorm ideas. Before I brainstorm, I decide ahead of time that I will not criticize any ideas until after I have finished brainstorming. I should be kind to myself and respect myself. I find that a tremendous amount of creativity explodes in a safe environment.

An atmosphere of safety can only be nurtured through love. 1 Corinthians 13:4-7 says, "Love is patient, Love is kind. It does not envy, it does not boast, it is not proud. It is not rude, it is not self-seeking, it is not easily angered, it keeps no account of wrongs. Love takes no pleasure in evil, but rejoices in the truth. It bears all things, believes all things, hopes all things, endures all things." I believe it is impossible to love without first loving Jesus Christ.

My authority as father and husband is granted to me as I submit to the lordship of Christ. The role of husband and father is not to be abused by using force or intimidation; using fear to establish obedience nullifies one's authority; using fear voids authority. Authority can only be given by God—humility is key to exercising authority.

I don't need to try and be a father or husband—those roles naturally flow out of my submission to Christ. The roles are always present, whereas the authority is gained or lost depending on my relationship to Jesus Christ. It becomes damaging, awkward, and neurotic when someone tries to generate authority on their own out of selfish ambition. God will not honor such men or women. A person becomes a brute when they try to force their way on the world; they become tyrannical.

Many well-meaning people can be brutish. The road to hell is paved with good intentions. Being good and self-righteous is not enough—you must be surrendered to Jesus Christ if you want to do good for your fellow man. Many well-meaning church leaders have caused more destruction than a hell-bent rebel. In the Bible, Jesus was gentle with people who were weak, but Jesus had hard words for the legalistic that were strong and self-righteous. It was the church leaders that had Jesus arrested, tortured, and killed. The Pharisees were convinced they were good people—they believed they were the best kind of people.

Being surrendered to Jesus Christ is the only way to be a part of the solution in the world; it allows Jesus to spread his mercy through you and into the world. Jesus will use us either way, whether we are surrendered or not. God is working his will through all things—although, in order to experience the peace and blessings of Christ, one must be surrendered to his lordship. People will prosper in a loving and safe environment—I have found this to be true.

CHAPTER 26

Finding a New Life

When starting a relationship with Jesus Christ, we are being introduced to a completely new perspective on life—it is a new journey. It is far different than what we are familiar with. It can be scary; one begins to trust in the invisible. We no longer live only by sight and experience. It is trusting that when you fall again, this time will be different because God is there to catch you.

Our old ways are terrible and filled with fear and strife. Relying on Jesus, for many, is a last-ditch effort in a state of despair. People are assailed with crushing loss and disappointment. Broken, they cry out to the endless sky for the stranger, Jesus, to save them. Most people are tired of trying to do life on their own terms when they decide to surrender to Jesus Christ; a long line of broken dreams lies in their wake.

We should stop trying to bushwhack our way through life and begin to let Jesus tell us how to live. The heart can be deceiving if we do not temper it with scripture; the heart will call us back to the destructive behaviors that hurt us in the first place. As bad as it was in the past, we are still tempted to try the old ways again. Proverbs 26:11 says, "As a dog returns to its vomit, so fools repeat their folly."

Why do I return to the bad things if they are actually bad? Doesn't that mean they are good because it's helping me survive? If Jesus is so good, then why do I run away from him? I find I want to run back to the old sins because they are familiar—I can remember the pain, but what comforts me is that it is familiar. Familiar is a powerful drug; familiar feels safe because, at the very least, I know what's going to happen. Jesus could be a lie. What if Jesus is not real? I will end up in an even worse place than when I started. It's terrifying to follow Jesus at times, especially when it's a brand-new road.

Matthew 16:25 says, "For whoever wants to save their life will lose it, but whoever loses their life for my sake will find it." I must let go of the old in order to grab something new. I have been asked to do this countless times in my life—learning to trust Jesus has become a lifestyle for me. As trust has been built, I begin to believe in Jesus more.

It is a relationship, not a set of principles or religious dogma to follow. It has nothing to do with discipline and everything to do with surrender—believing in Jesus is not enough. James 2:19 says, "You believe that there is one God. Good! Even the demons believe that—and shudder." It's not enough that I believe in God—the devil believes in God—what sets a person apart is when they put their trust in Jesus Christ; this requires a surrendered life and a contrite heart.

I have lost friends, family, ambitious goals, and moments of fleeting euphoria to follow Jesus, but I have also gained a sense of peace and satisfaction that I could not achieve before. I have new values. I never valued marriage and children in the past—I thought family was the problem. I didn't want family because I saw the pain and disappointment it brought. I was abused in a family, so I saw family as part of the problem.

Now, I understand that even good things will lead me to the road of death when I don't let God go before me. Family and children were not the problem—I despised the idea of having a family of my own because I saw what happened to my birth family. My father and mother certainly didn't follow Jesus, so they made a mess. The problem was living a life not following Jesus. My parents were fools because they decided to scorn Jesus and live life by their own power.

Living life on my own is choosing fantasy; it is choosing to chase my desires. At first it is very exciting to have an adventure into the unknown. Whether I chase relationships, sex, money, a worthy cause, or power...just fill in the blank with whatever it is that gets you excited—the Bible warns that these roads lead to death. There are two deaths: there is spiritual death and there is death when the body dies.

There are many multimillionaires walking around dead inside—they are smiling on the outside but dead as a grave on the inside. There is nothing wrong with millions of dollars, but what's the point if you are not alive inside?

By choosing to make Jesus my Lord, I have chosen to have a true perspective on life. I have chosen to see both the good and the bad, together, at the same time. I refuse to allow myself to be captured by fruitless pursuits. Jesus allows me to see the world for what it is.

When I submit to Jesus, I see a very different world. I see a world that is broken. It forces me to slow down and think about my own mortality. It is terrifying to see my limitations—my limitations fill me with dread. I find self-hatred, and I find that self-hatred drives me to drown myself with achievements—achievements that promise to make me feel like God if they are attained.

I feel pathetic, clumsy, and limited. I see that I am in need of a savior. It becomes obvious that I am not capable of saving myself from myself. I have feelings of helplessness and powerlessness—these are the worst feelings in the world; these are the feelings that are driving me with madness into an uncertain future. Life becomes a pursuit of empty vanity, hounded by death in a world without Jesus. The world rewards those who are able to distract themselves from the truth. The truth is that mankind was doomed the moment they decided to become gods themselves back in the Garden of Eden. Mankind has been hating their limitations and hating God from the beginning.

Human beings will do whatever it takes to push the reality of God out of their minds—no one wants to be reminded that they are a part of the problem. No one is good; we are all in bondage to sin in need of a savior. In reality, we are clumsy, cruel creatures that are scared out of our minds. We will do whatever it takes to win, no matter who gets stepped on. We all want to forget that we are needy and incapable of saving ourselves.

I find myself chasing after idols to forget that I am in a world that is being punished by God. When I stop trying to medicate myself with visions of grandeur...I see a suffering world in need.

The good news is that I can find peace in this world; I can be a part of the solution. The only way to be a part of the solution is for me to take responsibility for myself. I cannot take responsibility for Adam and Eve's first sin, but I can make a better choice than they did. I can choose to return to my creator, stop playing God, and start to rebuild. I can join with God and find my rightful place in the universe; I can find peace through Jesus Christ.

CHAPTER 27

Work Is a Gift from God

As far back as I can remember, I have struggled with exhaustion. When I was in first grade, my mother would splash cold water on my face to get me to the bus stop. I had a difficult time waking up in the morning, and staying on a routine has been impossible. I still struggle with exhaustion today.

I believe it must have to do with experiencing violence and humiliation by my father and neglect from my mother. My earliest memories are of my father coming home at lunchtime every day to beat me and call me worthless—this went on in my preschool years.

I believe the exhaustion has become chronic because it happened as a child when my brain was forming. For years I had to call on adrenaline rushes to find energy—I was either crashing or hypervigilant; there was no resting state for me.

I found that I was unable to keep a steady job. I am a sprinter when it comes to work; I am not a long-distance runner. I could only do work that didn't require a routine—I could do projects.

I was able to get an undergraduate degree in journalism and a master's degree in psychology because most of the work is done on my own time. I am proud of my degrees.

I was devastated that I could not keep a long term job. The world is not kind to those with weaknesses. I did my best with what I had. When I attempted a long term job I would put in my two weeks' notice when I saw that I could not sustain the work any longer.

I have noticed that many people use working like a drug—they will use work to avoid the responsibilities in their life. I have seen people overwork to medicate their own hurts. Overworking has destroyed families.

Overworking is rewarded in the culture. It is seen as a virtue to be a workaholic. Overworking covers all your sins in the world's eyes—it is seen as a badge of honor. People medicate with overworking while their lives slip down into the abyss of meaninglessness. Overworking destroys lives. Like alcoholism or addiction to drugs, workaholics medicate themselves rather than taking responsibility for their lives.

Hitler created death camps to systematically murder his enemies. Above the gateway, as a person entered the death camp, it read: "Arbeit macht frei." This translates as, "Work will set you free." The Nazis clearly exalted work above everything else. Their idolatry of work ended in death.

Work is a gift from God and can be a blessing. It can also be the very thing that keeps you from experiencing a meaningful life. Overworking to avoid responsibility is destructive and the road to death—many lives lay in a wasteland because they used work to avoid relationships.

I am still unable to keep a steady routine. I am healed in every way except for some physical pain and my inability to go to sleep and wake up at the same time every day.

My dad broke me when I was a child, and I have been broken ever since. I have healed much of the psychological damage, yet my body is hypersensitive to excitement. My body gets exhausted whether I am doing something fun or something stressful—it can be exasperating.

Writing is my outlet in a world hemmed in by exhaustion. I can write anytime, day or night. I have stacks of journals from over the years. I poured my hurts into journals in an effort to organize my struggles. I didn't hold back—I have been honest and bold in my writings.

For many years I believed what my dad said about me. He called me a lazy bum because I was tired much of the time. I didn't understand that he is what created my problem. I wrongly believed that I must be the problem; I thought that I was a lazy jerk that was trying to make people miserable.

I have always struggled with not being able to work, so writing has been a good outlet for me. I dedicated my life to overcoming the abuse I suffered; I used journaling to organize my thoughts. I was able to tie down the luggage that was banging around inside my head. Writing helped me to constructively dismantle the chaos. Now, I am sharing the specific things that helped me to overcome the child abuse. I hope to share my experience with others so they can be encouraged to fight for themselves—I want to help others understand how I found meaning in a meaningless world; I want to share exactly how Jesus Christ rescued me.

CHAPTER 28

Strength in Humility

As a child I felt powerless—I was helpless to save myself from my gigantic father. I was overpowered by the abuse. As I grew older, I gravitated toward strength. My favorite superhero was the Incredible Hulk. I would consume *Conan the Barbarian* comic books. I also watched all of the black and white *Godzilla* films. Godzilla was huge. I liked to pretend I was Godzilla, smashing the evil monsters who were intent on taking over the world.

I was also *Conan the Barbarian*, fighting evil and killing monsters. As Conan, I would go to foul places to kill evil monsters. Sometimes I would take on a band of murderers, rapists, and thieves in my imaginary world. I would rescue villagers from oppression. I became obsessed with physical strength—I had to become bigger and stronger so no one could ever overpower me again. Conan is a very dark comic, especially the *Savage Sword of Conan* series. While other children were watching *Mr. Rogers' Neighborhood*, I was more familiar with the violence of Conan—this shows the loss of my childhood and innocence.

I loved the old World War II movies where the Allies took on the evil Axis. The Americans were saving the world from tyranny; brave soldiers were willing to do whatever it took to stop the bullies. I loved war movies where evil would be destroyed and justice would be served. I admired the war heroes that put their lives on the line for freedom's sake.

Church was not inspiring at all to me. Church seemed to be more of a fairytale than the *Savage Sword of Conan*. *Conan the Barbarian* had more application to my life than church. I dreaded church for the most part—church was boring; there was no application. I was in crisis—gluing Popsicle sticks and cotton balls together seemed meaningless. Bible school was mostly crafts and singing about things I didn't understand.

I wanted to be strong, and everything I did in church looked weak. I couldn't wait to get home, where I could escape to my local creek and play Conan, *Star Wars*, or the Incredible Hulk. I was being abused at home, so church seemed meaningless.

I never saw the church as a place to go to for help as I got older. I heard a lot of platitudes and cliches—saying "Jesus loves you" has no meaning if you don't know who Jesus is. My parents were strangely obsessed with being at church every Sunday. I was experiencing hell at home, and then I would go to church where people were smiling and being nice to each other. Ninety percent of the time I was at home living in a world of violence and neglect; the other ten percent I was in a surreal world at church.

At school and at home, "being nice" got me hurt. At home I was being violently abused and terrorized. At school, kids would take my toys and refuse to give them back; I was being bullied at school.

There was violence everywhere. Church wasn't helpful; church felt fake to me. It wasn't the real world I was living in. As a child, church was a boring world where nothing was interesting.

I was told being good is the most noble pursuit. I was told to obey my parents and to be good; I tried being good but that didn't stop the beatings at home. When I was being good at school, it made me a target for bullies—being good kept me submissive and obedient to bullies. Being good didn't change my father's opinion about me; being good didn't stop the beatings at home or the bullying at school. I was never convinced that being good was going to help at all.

Church was a place where people would be good to each other only on Sunday—the rest of the week was only about survival. Sundays were where people would talk about being good. I wanted nothing to do with being good—I didn't want to be bad, but I knew I couldn't be good. Being good kept me weak.

Being good is wishful thinking; being good is how hopeless people medicate themselves against the truth. The truth is that people are horribly selfish and they don't care who they hurt to get what they want. Being good is a weakling's fantasy contrived out of feelings of powerlessness at best. Predators rule in a world where being good is the highest of virtues. I was told, as a child, that being good is what God wants from me—they got it dead wrong. Romans 3:10-12: "None is righteous, no, not one; no one understands; no one seeks for God. All have turned aside; together they have become worthless; no one does good, not even one."

Being good is the same as being weak—good people are weak people. I have learned that a good person can't get into heaven. Jesus is not looking for good people; God brings good into the world, not people.

Jesus is looking for broken people. Jesus wants humble people that are aware that they are flawed beings. A truly strong person recognizes his limitations and makes the adjustments necessary. A truly strong person recognizes their weakness and admits they are weak. The apostle Paul wrote in 2 Corinthians 12:9-10: "But he said to me, 'My grace is sufficient for you, for my power is perfected in weakness.' Therefore I will boast all the more gladly in my weaknesses, so that the power of Christ may rest on me. That is why, for the sake of Christ, I delight in weaknesses, in insults, in hardships, in persecutions, in difficulties. For when I am weak, then I am strong."

Surrendering to Jesus is the *only* true strong act a person can do. If a man is to be effective, he must learn to recognize his weaknesses. Every strong man has a weak spot—it is weak to overcompensate for limitations by being scary, by lying, by cheating, by stealing, etc.... Stoicism is another way that weak men avoid taking responsibility.

On the surface, stoicism seems like a great idea. Stoicism is the endurance of pain or hardship without the display of feelings and without complaint. Stoicism is being silent in the face of hardship. I believe that too many women and men are silent in hardship. Relationships require communication to survive; being silent destroys relationships. Being stoic is seen as a virtue to the world—I see stoicism destroying the world with silence. It is doing nothing under the flag of virtue.

Being stoic is how a man avoids engaging the relationships in his life. A coward is stoic because stoicism is a shortcut. Being stoic is being silent. It takes courage to engage an uncomfortable conversation; it takes courage to wrestle through relationship problems where our natural tendency is to run away when the heat gets turned up.

Being stoic is the sin of omission, and both men and women can equally be guilty of stoicism, although stoicism seems to be a virtue among men. When a person sees evil being done, and when they do nothing, they are guilty of being morally weak. Edmund Burke famously said: "The only thing necessary for evil to triumph in the world is that good men do nothing."

I was being told to be a pacifist by the church, which also marries comfortably with stoicism. Stoicism seems to be a virtue for both the church and the culture. I believe this thinking has castrated conservative men. Stoicism shuts down the conversations that need to take place. Stoicism says to be strong and silent—I say be strong but *don't* be silent.

As a young man, I was told that stoicism is strong. I found that stoicism only made things worse. I could not engage the lies of the culture with silence. I continued to get overpowered by very loud, evil people, that were all too happy for me to be stoic.

Strength is found in submission to Jesus Christ. Strength is in a man or woman submitting to Jesus Christ and looking upon themselves with sober eyes. Strength is not found in being the good person or the lawful person—strength is found in humility. Humility is strength under control. A wild stallion is strong, but a trained warhorse is stronger. Strength comes from submission to God and *only* God.

Overexaggerating your capabilities puts you at risk. It is good to have courage, but it is better to have discernment—discernment is learned through seeing the world for what it is, not for what you want it to be. Discernment comes through taking an honest inventory of yourself and your capabilities. Courage alone is not enough—you can be courageous and ineffective; it's better to apply humility before courage.

I had a tremendous amount of courage when I was young but I did not have discernment. I have learned discernment through submitting to Jesus Christ. I am now a strong man because I love Jesus first.

Being dishonest with yourself or others makes you weak. Dishonesty is being immoral, and immorality is weak character—nothing strong can be done when a person has bad character.

Good character is when strength and weakness are accounted for and the proper adjustments have been made. Wisdom can only be exercised from a person who is humble and has accounted for their limitations. Wisdom is knowing when to apply knowledge—a person can be smart but not wise.

Again, the apostle Paul said in 2 Corinthians 12:10, "That is why, for the sake of Christ, I delight in weaknesses, in insults, in hardships, in persecutions, in difficulties. For when I am weak, then I am strong." Paul was wise because he understood that he was a created being that needed to be back in union with his creator to be effective in life. Being good doesn't make one strong—being humble makes a person strong.

CHAPTER 29

FREE WILL

Why is God hidden? Why does God make it impossible to prove he exists without question? If God loves us, why does he play hide-and-seek all the time? Why would God make it so difficult to know him if he loves us so much? If God hurts when we hurt, then why does God hide from us?

Isn't God being cruel by playing games? Is God gaslighting us when he makes us question our own sanity because we can't find him? If God loves us so much, why does he hide from us?

These are all very good questions that deserve a thoughtful and rational response. I have come to understand that everything good comes from God: a sunset, taste from food, medicine, love, beauty—anything you can think of that is good comes from God. On the contrary, bad comes from humans and their ancestors from the beginning.

Humans brought suffering on themselves when Adam and Eve rebelled against God. Unfortunately, we have all inherited Adam and Eve's world. We entered into a world that has already been broken by sin. We are not guilty of Adam and Eve's sin, but we did inherit a world where there is opportunity to sin. It is inevitable that we will all sin—we are born into a world where the temptation to sin is too great. Like Adam and Eve, we will eventually sin as well.

It doesn't seem fair that we inherit Adam and Eve's problems until you look a little closer. I have come to understand why we inherit Adam and Eve's curse. God allowed Adam and Eve the opportunity to sin so that we could make a choice to follow him—I don't believe that God wanted robots.

God created human beings and allowed for evil so we could have the privilege of a choice. God gave us free will—that is what makes us different than anything else in creation. Animals do not have free will; animals have instincts. We are remarkable because we have free will. We can choose to love God or deny him. God loves us so much that he is risking rejection. If you love something, set it free. God gave us the freedom to reject him. God wants us to want him. God desires an authentic relationship with us; God doesn't force himself on us.

Hell is for eternity. Hell is where people choose to go that don't want to follow God. They get to live eternity in a place where there is no God. Hell is not literally fire and brimstone—it is simply a place without God; a place without love and creativity. It is a place devoid of hope where everything stays the same forever. Hell is a place full of narcissistic people, where everyone is demanding to be served but no one is willing to serve, and this goes on for eternity.

Hell is a place separate from God—no beauty, no love, no relationship—only self, forever. Hell is a place where you thirst and never get a drink. It is where you are hungry and never get food. You try to feel good but it always ends in frustration. There are people that would rather live in hell than be present with God. Hell is locked from the inside. An evil person's transition into hell begins on Earth, in this lifetime—some people would rather stand in the rain than be in a warm home with someone they don't like.

Evil comes from a collected, concerted effort by human beings and their selfish ambition to control others. Doing evil is what separates mankind from God. Of course, the devil is working against human beings as well—the devil and all of his demons are doing everything in their power to fill up hell. I believe that God allows Satan to exist because Satan gives people another master to follow. Humans need a master because they are created beings, and the devil is the alternative choice from God.

We are all subject to our own propensity to worship. We are created beings, so we look for things to worship. We will always worship—we will either worship ourselves, which is following the devil, or we will worship God.

I have come to understand that God is not hidden; the problem is that mankind cannot see God because our sin corrupts us. Sin blinds us from seeing God.

I believe God is all around us but we don't see him because we live in a muddy world. The water isn't clear anymore—it has been muddied by humans and their sin. The problem lies with us. Mankind's selfish ambition has blocked the signal with God. We get bad reception with God because we are blinded by sin.

I see God more and more as I walk with him. The muddy water begins to clear up as I surrender daily and over time. As I build trust with God, I get more insight into God. God allowed for us to go our own way, but he also gave us a way back through Jesus Christ. God came into our sick, dying world to save us from ourselves. God is willing to clear up our eyes to see him if we will allow him to lead us. God empathizes with us and desires us to return to him. He is the good father that won't force us to follow him.

We are God's greatest creation. We are God's masterpiece, according to Ephesians 2:10: "For we are God's masterpiece. He has created us anew in Christ Jesus, so we can do the good things he planned for us long ago."

CHAPTER 30

DON'T WORRY

I don't have to be an expert on anything in order to navigate the world, whether it's who to vote for or what I believe about climate change. I have learned to ask myself one question: Is fear driving me?

Fear can be very good because it alerts me to things that might be harmful to me. Fear is not necessarily a bad thing—fear can be good if it moves me to safety. Fear keeps me from driving too fast or taking unnecessary chances. Fear can be my friend, as long as I stay focused on Jesus.

Fear can also be destructive—fear can turn into terror and panic, if I allow myself to be overcome. Fear can be my ally or it can be my enemy. Fear can trigger me into a state where I am no longer thinking but only reacting. Fear can turn me into a panicking animal that is easily led by evil people.

I know I am overreacting if a person or an ideology strikes fear into my heart and makes me worry. I have learned to see worrying as a red flag. When I find myself worrying, I stop everything I am doing and take a personal inventory of my thoughts.

When I am worrying, it means that I am playing God. I am trying to control the situation when I worry—God warns against worrying.

Worrying is when one ruminates on a tragic scenario. Worrying lies to you. Worrying tells you that if you stop thinking about your concern, then doom will follow. Worrying is a bully—it takes the joy out of life by dominating your thoughts. Most of the things I have worried about never came to pass. We don't have a choice on being afraid. We have a choice to not worry.

The best ways I have learned to deal with worry is to take action or to surrender my fear to Jesus. I take action if I have the ability to do so. I can sit around and worry about who is going to be the next president or I can go and vote. Voting helps me to know that I have done my part—I do everything I can and leave the rest up to God.

If I feel a responsibility to act and I don't act because of fear, then I will worry. Inaction exacts a terrible price. Cowardice is not kind to my conscience; cowardice eats away at the soul. Giving into fear dehumanizes a person; being a coward allows a tyranny to reign over your life that paralyzes you into submission. Shame will hang over you and oppress you. Shame is a terrible master. Cowardice steals your life and turns you into a slave of fear. Anxiety dominates where there is inaction. James 4:17 says, "If anyone, then, knows the good they ought to do and doesn't do it, it is a sin to them."

The other way to deal with worry is to surrender it to Jesus. If I have no control over what I am worried about, then I surrender it to God. I don't want to try and play God by assuming the outcome of a situation I have no control over. I do not own a crystal ball that tells me the future. Worrying about what could happen or might happen is an absolute waste of time. I pray over the situation then surrender it to God. I can't control the feeling of fear, but I can choose to focus on something more productive.

I run away from worrying—worrying must be dealt with aggressively and quickly or it will rage out of control. My favorite way to deal with worrying is to pray to God and surrender control to him. I resolve to do something if given the opportunity.

Worry can suddenly ambush me with a terrible image or a tragic scenario. Worry is always selling a future scenario; it is never a clear and present danger. If something is immediate, then it demands an immediate action. Worry is always warning about a tragic future. Worry is a liar—worry tries to convince you that you need it. Worry feeds off of you like a leech; it's a leech that feeds off of fear.

A good way to defeat worry is to look at the reality of the situation. Do not try to predict the outcome or you will fall victim to worry. Resist the urge to comfort yourself by predicting outcomes. I tell the worry: "I will cross that bridge when I get there."

Do not predict the future or dwell on past tragedies. Stand in the present; stand on the reality of the moment; stand on the truth. The Bible tells us to stand our ground against the enemy. Ephesians 6:13 says, "Therefore put on the full armor of God, so that when the day of evil comes, you may be able to stand your ground, and after you have done everything, to stand." To stand is mentioned twice in this verse. Don't attack; don't run—only stand.

Ephesians 6:16 says, "In addition to all this, take up the shield of faith, with which you can extinguish all the flaming arrows of the evil one." It mentions the shield of faith. Faith is trust in God to keep us safe. Faith is shown as a shield in this verse. A bow is not used in a close battle. A bow is a distance weapon. If the battle is close, we are to take immediate offensive action. If it is an attack from the distance, then we are to play defense. A shield is a defensive weapon. The flaming arrows are metaphors for evil thoughts or scenarios that ambush our mind from a distance. We are to play defense when worry attacks us; we hold up our shield of faith—we trust that God will protect us from the things we have no control over.

We can be tempted to believe that our faith isn't working when we see our shield full of arrows. It's scary to see a shield that looks like a porcupine. We can be tempted to throw away the shield in despair and give up.

Seeing a shield full of arrows can be scary—although, a shield full of arrows means that it is working—the arrows are being stopped short of their mark. Do not get discouraged and think you are losing when you see a shield crowded with arrows. It is tiring work to defend yourself. Don't mistake being exhausted for failure. You can be exhausted and still be winning. The devil wants us to lower our shield from discouragement so his arrows start hitting your heart. The heart is our will to continue and not give up—an arrow in the heart is a kill shot.

We are taken out of the fight when we give in to worry. We become paralyzed when fear takes hold. Fear can be our friend, but when it gives way to panic, we become paralyzed and easily led.

In the face of worry, we are called to take action; we take action by trusting in Jesus. Faith is not passive. The Bible says in Philippians 4:6-7: "Be anxious for nothing, but in everything, by prayer and petition, with thanksgiving, present your request to God. And the peace of God, which surpasses all understanding, will guard your hearts and minds in Christ Jesus."

The opposite of worry is peace. God promises peace to those who trust him. One can find peace in the midst of battle. Peace is trusting in God for the outcome no matter what our eyes are telling us—only God can give peace. I demote myself from creator to created. Peace comes when I let go and let God run the universe.

CHAPTER 31

EMPATHY

I find that most people go through life living in a fantasy. The world can seem insane, because it *is* insane. The definition of insanity is doing the same thing over and over and expecting a different result each time. There are insane people all around us. If you don't believe the world is insane, then you haven't lived long enough to experience it. I find that when I refuse to trust God, I become an insane person, as well.

Science has brought wonderful achievements that have alleviated the suffering of humans everywhere. God has given us the gift of science. The universe is not chaos—the universe is able to be studied by science because there are predictable patterns. The universe is finely tuned. Science is impossible in a chaotic universe; science is a miracle, but science is not God.

Modern humans tend to mock ancient civilizations because they did not have the scientific achievements we had today. I would argue that people haven't changed at all from the beginning. Science is distracting us from the fact that we are still depraved and broken. We can cure many diseases and alleviate suffering, but we also use gain-of-function research to create biological weapons to destroy life.

Scientific achievement is used as a distraction—it does not solve the problem of aging and death. Science is God until you find you have an incurable disease. Death is the ultimate incurable disease. Scientific discovery is wonderful, but it also can be used as a dangerous fantasy. It is a wonderful tool we have to alleviate human suffering, but it does not solve the ultimate questions to meaning and purpose.

Science is wonderful, but it gets abused like a drug is abused. Painkillers are a miracle, but if you live for painkillers, your life becomes meaningless and without purpose—this culture relies far too heavily on scientific achievements to answer the most difficult questions about pain and suffering.

Science is overrated when used incorrectly. Science becomes pseudoscience when it is used to answer life's bigger questions. Even our most brilliant scientists are guilty of insanity when they use science to give us meaning and purpose. There are people that can split the atom and there are people that can slam dunk a basketball—both of these things are amazing, but neither are good for bringing meaning and purpose to the world.

I am not picking on science here. Money, marriage, family values, drugs, serving, sex, power…all can be substituted for science in my scenario. Many good things can distract us from God. We have a tendency to worship the creation and not the creator.

Morality is the best indicator of progress. I measure human beings by their capacity for empathy. Empathy is the ability to understand and share the feelings of another. True change comes when a person begins to empathize for others.

Considerate is being careful not to cause inconvenience or hurt to others. *Thoughtful* is showing careful consideration for the needs of others. Giving relationships careful consideration and thoughtfulness requires empathy. When I surrendered to Jesus Christ and took responsibility for the pain I brought to the world, I began to have empathy. I was able to look at people and consider what they are going through. As I recognized my own capacity for evil, I was humbled. I closed my mouth and began to listen to others.

Most people believe they are good—this belief has brought a tremendous amount of destruction and pain to the world. For example, if a person believes money solves all of the problems of the world, then they would think it is good to eliminate those who cannot work. They would only give money to the strong and abandon the weak. The rich person would believe they are doing a good work in the world as they actually bring pain and destruction.

God is the only giver of good. We can surrender ourselves to be used by God to bring good into the world. God's perfect timing can only be known by God—I need to align myself with God to become effective in the world. Empathy is how I align my resources to become effective in the world.

People who covet money and power always ignore human rights. They are taking a shortcut to their desires—rather than taking the time needed to protect relationships, they look for ways to get what they want, regardless of human suffering. They use people to get stuff rather than using stuff to serve people.

Most people claim their cause is good so they can justify their own selfish ambition. In the name of good, they bring about destruction and suffering. Romans 3:12 says, "All have turned away, they have together become worthless; there is no one who does good, not even one."

Empathy brings about a good solution for everyone—everyone wins. It's the best-case scenario. Empathy comes from love and Jesus Christ is love.

Jesus Christ has shown us love by coming to Earth as a man to save us from ourselves. God became man so that he could reach us. God empathized with us by becoming flesh and suffering in the world we live in. God knows what it is like to be us by his becoming us in the man Jesus Christ.

Jesus Christ is a personal God; he is a relationship. Jesus Christ tells us what real meaning and purpose are. We are able to love because God first loved us. We would be forever lost in darkness if Jesus had not come down from heaven to help us. Man's attempt to be good always ends in death and destruction.

1 Corinthians 13:1-3 says:

If I speak in the tongues of men and of angels, but have not love, I am only a ringing gong or a clanging cymbal. If I have the gift of prophecy and can fathom all mysteries and all knowledge, and if I have absolute faith so as to move mountains, but have not love, I am nothing. If I give all I possess to the poor and exult in the surrender of my body, but have not love, I gain nothing.

God is love.

CHAPTER 32

Familiar Words

Because of the violent world I was born into I desperately searched for pursuits that would validate my existence—I had been dehumanized with violence and condemned by abandonment.
I had no love for family. I had no understanding of good—I didn't trust good. I didn't believe happiness was attainable. My world was defined by crushing grief. I was hopeless. I found comfort in songs about fear and sadness—loneliness, fear, and rejection were my friends. Love was a fairytale that I couldn't afford.

I was alone. My life was a crisis. I was a shell of a man making my way through the wasteland. I was surviving and I knew nothing else. I knew in my heart that I would never thrive, but then God spoke to me.

The God of everything good managed to speak to me in a way that I could understand him. God is love and I was in a world of hate and apathy. What could God possibly say to me that I would listen to?

In one of my many moments of despair, I decided to open the Bible. I began to read, only I was astonished at what I read. I had opened to the book of Ecclesiastes.

In Ecclesiastes 1:1-2, it says, "The words of the teacher, son of David, king in Jerusalem: 'Meaningless! Meaningless!' says the teacher. 'Utterly meaningless! Everything is meaningless.'" The verses went on to say how everything man does is meaningless and pointless—this got my attention because I too felt that way. I believed everything is meaningless.

The book of Ecclesiastes was written by King Solomon. King Solomon was the richest and most powerful man of his time. He had every desire at his disposal, yet this powerful man is crying out to God how everything is meaningless except the pursuit of God.

I didn't know anything about King Solomon. I didn't see the Bible as an authoritative source at the time. My experience with Christianity, up to that point, was being told that I need to be good if I want to be happy. I knew that being good wasn't going to help me—most of the good people I knew were weak people. I had no interest in being a nice but weak person.

What caught my attention is that the Bible was saying the opposite of what Christians were saying to me. The Bible was contradicting Christians. The Christians I knew, at the time, saw me as an antagonist and troublemaker when I despaired. I was accused of being selfish and evil because of my questions about God. I can see now that I was talking to immature Christians.

Ecclesiastes reads like a heavy metal song—it spoke to the pain in my soul. I was intrigued about following God because it affirmed my experience that everything else is meaningless. I had not tried to follow God. I dove into Christian apologetics, theology, and philosophy. I was hoping that I was wrong about everything being meaningless.

My pursuit of meaning into Christianity has not come back empty. I learned about Jesus Christ who was all-good and came to earth to tell us good news. Jesus was good and he was tortured and murdered for this—that made sense to me. I lived in a world where only the strong survive and the weak were crushed under the weight of injustice.

God brought meaning into my life; God gave me hope that life had purpose. I never believed in justice until I saw that Jesus suffered like I had. Jesus showed empathy when he suffered on my behalf.

My hurts were real—I could no longer push them aside through stoicism. I was broken. I was lost. Jesus solved my dilemma at the cross. How could I get back the years that were stolen from me by violence and neglect? Who is outraged about my pain? Who cares for a lost and lonely loser like me? I was abandoned by my parents and the world only sought to hurt me. Jesus understood my pain; Jesus became my advocate—Jesus is an advocate for the hated and abandoned.

CHAPTER 33

KNOWING IS HALF THE BATTLE

I made a promise to myself in high school—I promised myself to solve the big questions of life; I was determined to make an impact. I wasn't considering God. God wasn't in my thoughts. I didn't have a problem with religion, but I never considered it as a part of the solution either. I didn't give religion a second thought.

I saw that my family was fake and that I was fake. I didn't want to be a pretentious person. I started striving for authenticity. I set some goals in front of me and gave them everything I had.

I had courage and heart; I was bold and brave. I believed that I could be whatever I wanted to be. I didn't let anyone stand in the way of my dreams and I set lofty goals. I outworked my peers. I worked hard—I hustled. I did all the things that I knew that it took to be a man—a real man. I was fearless. It got me nowhere.

I followed the world's prescription on how to be a successful man. I did all of the cliche things I was told to do by the culture—all of the hype about how a man should live simply didn't work.

Unfortunately, I had no foundation in my life. I was flying completely blind. I had no idea what I was doing. I had no help or safety net if I fell. I was confused about what was important; I had no clear picture of what success looked like. I was still dealing with exhaustion. My feelings of inadequacy were regular tsunamis that I had to survive; I was having nightmares from the violence I suffered. I was exhausted from being terrified. I was a ship without a compass. I had no parents that gave me safety or direction. I was trying to overcompensate for the hopelessness and powerlessness that assailed me daily. I was battling abuse and I didn't even know it.

I was battling all the things a child would be battling if he were born in a haunted house—there was terror, nightmares, despair, hopelessness, and powerlessness. I felt disillusioned with life, disconnected. I felt that I had been shattered in a million pieces; I had no center.

Shattered is the best word I have to describe how I felt. I had no clue how badly I had been abused before I opened that book—I didn't know what I was dealing with. I thought my problem was that I was weak. In reality, I was reacting normally to an abnormal situation.

In my heart, I knew that something was wrong with me—I wasn't like everyone else. I assumed my dad was right about me when he said that I would never amount to anything and then followed that up with a violent beating. I thought my dad beat me hard and called me a loser because there was something wrong with me. I thought my failure to make it in life was because I was cursed.

I finally started to peek into a book about child abuse when I was a senior in college. I found a book for men about child abuse. I held onto it out of curiosity, but I was terrified to read it. The book read like my journal—finally something made sense to me. I was horrified by what I read and by the realization of what had happened to me. It was my worst nightmare come true. I came to the realization that I was different than other people; I was broken.

It was extremely painful to read the book, but my desire to overcome this monster drove me forward. After reading the book, I had satisfaction that I knew what my problem was; at the same time, I was horrified to discover that I was broken. I figured out what was wrong with me, while at the same time, I felt the death of all my hopes and dreams.

The book was right about what had happened to me, but I found little hope in the book. It said positive things, but I could tell that I was beyond the help of the book. It was an excellent book at describing my nightmare, but its solutions did not resonate with me. I know now that the book wasn't helpful because it didn't have a helpful solution.

In hindsight, I am grateful for the book because it showed me that I was abused; the book helped me break my denial. It started me on my journey to taking the violence and neglect I suffered as a child seriously.

After I finished the book, I found myself teetering on the edge of a deep abyss in my mind. My eyes were opened and I saw myself shattered beyond repair. I found myself stuck in a deep well with no escape—my search to find answers to this abuse had begun. The book started the darkest time in my life.

Intellectual giant and Christian writer, C.S. Lewis wrote: "Pain insists upon being attended to. God whispers to us in our pleasures, speaks in our consciences, but shouts in our pains. It is his megaphone to rouse a deaf world."

CHAPTER 34

The Armor of God

I have always admired power and strength—I want to be strong. The Bible shares in Ephesians 6:10-20 on how to be strong by putting on "the full armor of God." The Full Armor of God passage in the Bible is used as a metaphor on how to stand up against the evil spiritual forces that threaten to destroy us. There is an invisible spiritual battle being waged for our souls.

In verse 10 it says I am to "be strong in the Lord." I cannot be strong by myself; I must seek to put God first in everything I do. I am to bring my desires to the Lord first before I execute them; I am to ask God for direction. I can do this by praying and listening for God to speak to me through my conscience.

I will consult the Bible topically. I look for the themes that are relevant to my desires in the Scripture. I may also seek counsel from a Christian authority that I respect. I have learned to be careful with my desires by being patient and seeking direction.

In the past, I put more attention toward physical strength. I love watching The World's Strongest Man competitions or Mixed Martial Arts. Physical strength is ok, but a truly strong man understands that there is a spiritual realm—to be adequately prepared to navigate a hostile world, I must be well-rounded. What good is it to be physically strong if you are easily deceived? Physical strength is good, but spiritual strength is better.

There are dark forces intent upon destroying our lives that are actively set against us; there are good forces we can access by surrender and submission to Jesus Christ. I cannot escape having a master—the fool believes that he answers to no one.

What a person desires most also becomes their limitations. Whether you are spiritual or not, it is a universal truth that whatever you love the most also becomes your master. If you love money, then your life becomes limited by the limitations that money offers. Money does not know how to unlock the secrets to having a functional relationship with someone.

You can be a billionaire and also be an absolute fool on how to navigate relationships. I have noticed that most billionaire's personal lives are a mess—they have been married several times and they can't find personal happiness in relationships; they have tremendous spending power, yet happiness cannot be found if you don't know how to solve loneliness. It is good to be rich, but money doesn't solve everything—that is one example out of endless examples of how I must be careful with what I let my heart pursue. The invisible world must be taken seriously.

The armor of God is a metaphor in the Bible that helps me to understand how I am protected when I seek Jesus Christ first in everything. The armor is made up of a belt, breastplate, shoes, shield, helmet, and sword. In the next few chapters I will break down each piece of the armor to show how it specifically relates to real life.

CHAPTER 35

BELT OF TRUTH

The belt of truth is what holds your pants up. Ephesians 6:14 states: "Stand firm then, with the belt of truth buckled around your waist..." You don't want your pants falling down in battle—you can't fight with your pants around your ankles. The belt also holds your sword and other gear; the belt keeps your clothing in place.

I am a seeker. I have dedicated my life to searching for what is true. Like a drowning person, I clutch for what can hold me up above the water. Truth is my life jacket. I love the truth and I hate lies. Truth is what empowers me—I am hungry for what is true. The pursuit of truth has been changing me from a weak slave of fear and into a strong man. Truth is the cornerstone of my life; truth is the rare and precious fuel that powers the engines that run my life.

I believe scripture is truth. I believe the Bible is God-inspired, like it says. I have found the Bible to be the greatest book I have ever read. Again, 2 Timothy 3:16-17 says, "All scripture is God-breathed and is useful for teaching, rebuking, correcting, and training in righteousness so that the servant of God may be thoroughly equipped for every good work." Scripture is special because it is the actual words of God—it is not a book about God, but a book written by God. I have found this to be true as I grow with Christ.

The Scripture has proved itself to be true throughout my life. When I was young, I didn't understand that the invisible world is more important than the visible world. I have learned to seek what the Bible says is good. I guard my heart from being stolen by lesser gods. I am finding that it is better to be a wise man than a rich man—being rich is good, but wisdom is best. Truth enables me to navigate the world and makes me stronger.

I do not pretend that I have it all figured out. I have found that truth grows like a light. The light was dim in the beginning, but I am able to see better and better as I go. I am a work in progress—I will get things wrong and fail from time to time, yet I won't be caught with my pants down when I have the belt of truth fastened around my waist. John 8:31-32 says, "Jesus said to the people who believed in him, 'You are truly my disciples if you remain faithful to my teachings. Then you will know the truth, and the truth will set you free.'"

The Bible is dangerous to tyranny. Tyrannical people hate that I am free. The Bible is a dangerous book to those that would like to rule over me. The truth has set me free—that makes me a dangerous man. A man should be both good and dangerous—dangerous to evildoers.

CHAPTER 36

Breastplate of Righteousness

The breastplate of righteousness is the next piece in the armor. Ephesians 6:14 says, "...with the breastplate of righteousness arrayed." The breastplate guards the heart. If my heart is pierced by a weapon, then there is instant death—I don't stand a chance if I do not believe I have any rights.

Righteousness is the quality of being morally right or justifiable. When the Bible speaks of being righteous, it means being *made* right.

I am not righteous by my own power. I was once a child of this world; I was unrighteous. I was a child of wrath according to the Bible. Ephesians 2:3 says, "All of us also lived among them at one time, gratifying the cravings of our flesh and following its desires and thoughts. Like the rest, we were by nature children of wrath."

Jesus made me righteous when he paid the price for my sins at the cross with his death. I am justified, which means to be declared or made righteous in the sight of God. I have been declared good by the King of Kings—I am no longer a slave to the lies that I am unworthy or hopeless.

Being righteous gives me the authority to look any man or woman in the face without shame. I can stand before a king with boldness—I have been made righteous by God. My failures and limitations do not define who I am. I am now a child of God and I have all the rights therein. My identity is in Christ. Romans 8:31 says, "What shall we say about such wonderful things as these? If God is for us, who can ever be against us?" When God is my advocate, I am unstoppable.

CHAPTER 37

Shoes of Peace

The shoes are the next piece of armor. Ephesians 6:15 says, "and with your feet fitted with the readiness of the gospel of peace." Soldiers need good shoes so they can plant their feet firmly on the ground. A good shoe, with grip, can mean the difference between life or death. Shoes need cleats if you are going to be throwing your weight around. Footwork and stance are everything in a sword fight or hand-to-hand combat—it's not good if you have shoes with no traction. One does not want to fall in a fight for your life.

The spiritual shoes the Bible is referring to here have to do with peace; I should seek peace in every confrontation. Peace is when I desire the best outcome for everyone when there is conflict. It is easy to let anger turn into rage and have a heart of revenge. I should never to try and humiliate my enemies; I do not want to return evil for evil.

The Bible says to "*stand* when the day of evil comes." Ephesians 6:13 says, "Therefore put on the full armor of God, so that when the day of evil comes, you may be able to *stand* your ground, and after you have done everything, to *stand*." Stand is emphasized here; it is mentioned twice. Do not attack in rage or retreat in terror—stand your ground.

It is wrong to attack out of revenge. At the same time, it is wrong to give in to terror and run. Attacking in rage throws me off balance; running away turns my back to the enemy—neither are a good choice. Both attacking and running away are weak responses. We are called to stand, not to attack or run away. When I make a *stand*, my feet are "...shod with the gospel of peace" according to Ephesians 6:15. Making a stand is always seeking peace in every confrontation.

To be a part of the solution in the world, I must seek peace. Seeking peace means that when I need to confront anyone, I do so with thoughtfulness and much consideration. I should never fly off the handle or lose my temper—there is a time to attack, but it should be a last resort, when all other methods have been exhausted.

Working toward peace in a confrontation keeps my wits about me. It is best to keep my head in a fight—seeking peace is being strong.

Pacifism has nothing to do with biblical peace; pacifism is not biblical. Being a pacifist means that use of force—or even deadly force—is never an option. Jesus was not advocating to be a pacifist. Jesus died on the cross as a sacrifice to pay for the sins of mankind. Jesus did not seek justice against his attackers because he came to be killed as a perfect sacrifice for the sins of mankind. John 1:36 says "and he looked at Jesus as he walked by and said, 'Behold the Lamb of God!" He is seen as a Lamb to be sacrificed. Jesus volunteered to be sacrificed; Jesus came to die on our behalf—that is not pacifism.

Pacifism is an ideology that condemns using deadly force to defend yourself against someone trying to murder you. Never kill anyone, at any cost, is the ideology of pacifism. On the other hand, Jesus advocates killing someone if they are trying to murder you. Jesus told his disciples in Luke 22:36, "'Now, however,' he told them, 'the one with a purse should take it, and likewise a bag; and the one without a sword should sell his cloak and buy one.'" Jesus knew that his disciples would need to protect themselves in the event of self-defense. Jesus being murdered on the cross has everything to do with being a perfect sacrifice for the sins of mankind and nothing to do with pacifism. Pacifism is a Buddhist concept and has nothing to do with Christianity.

The Ten Commandments have also been misquoted. The sixth commandment says, "You shall not murder." Many wrongfully believe that the Ten Commandments say, "You should not kill." Exodus 20:13 says, "You shall not murder." Murder is defined as "the unlawful premeditated killing of one human being by another." Killing is simply taking a life. Killing for the right reasons is acceptable to God. Murder is never acceptable.

I am a child of God—I have infinite value. If someone comes to murder me or my family, then I am called to use deadly force to stop them if necessary. Deadly force is a last resort after all other avenues have been exhausted. The spiritual shoes of peace ensure that I have exhausted every chance to bring peace into a situation. The spiritual shoes of peace do not allow me to return hate for hate—I should never allow hate in to my heart. Murder is wrong, whereas, having a peaceful mindset when using deadly force to stop a murderer is a noble pursuit indeed.

Seeking a peaceful resolution should be the chief aim in every confrontation; it ensures I will be blameless and pure before God. Psalm 34:14 says, "Turn from evil and do good. Search for peace, and work to maintain it."

CHAPTER 38

Shield of Faith

The next piece of armor is the shield of faith. A warrior's shield is used as cover to defend against blows from the enemies' weapons—the shield is used to block any incoming attacks. The shield is primarily a defensive weapon that is the first line of defense. Ephesians 6:16 says, "In addition to all this, take up the shield of faith, with which you can extinguish all the flaming arrows of the evil one."

Faith is the spiritual word emphasized here. The word faith can be used the same as trust—faith simply means trust.

The devil will attack Christians by trying to convince them they are bad. Shame is the weapon Satan uses to kill; shame says there is no hope for you—this passage specifically uses arrows as the weapon of choice because arrows are a distance weapon. Attacks come to me in the form of accusations. Feelings of hopelessness and shame try to derail me to give up on life; Satan wants to take me out of the battle.

Feelings of hopelessness have caused me to consider suicide in the past. The flaming arrows came, relentlessly trying to destroy me. The arrows would say, "Why keep going through so much pain? Why bother? I am going to lose! I am a loser. Everything in my life says I am a loser. I cannot escape this—I am hopeless; I am no good; I can't win; I am cursed."

The arrows came relentlessly and mercilessly. I could believe these lies or I could have faith in what God says about me. I can trust that God is right when he calls me his child. I can believe that Jesus bought me and grafted me into his family. I am now in the family lineage of royalty. The God of the universe has spoken and declares me righteous—I am free.

Sometimes the shield can be filled with arrows and I will feel like I am losing because of so many arrows. I want to give up out of exhaustion. By faith, I surrender in those moments to God. God will fight my battles for me. I rest in Jesus and hold aloft my shield of trust, never letting it down.

In these exhausted times, I remember not to try and defeat the accusations with my own strength, but to surrender to Jesus Christ. When I am exhausted, it is helpful to remember that it doesn't matter if I am exhausted because I don't need to feel strong to win. I can allow the exhaustion to let me collapse into God's arms by surrendering. It is not by my strength that I fight my battles, but by surrendering and letting God fight for me. The shield is telling me that I need to trust in Jesus and the arrows will never hit me. Isaiah 41:10 says, "So do not fear, for I am with you; do not be dismayed, for I am your God. I will strengthen you and help you; I will uphold you with my righteous right hand."

CHAPTER 39

Helmet of Salvation

Ephesians 6:17 says, "Take the helmet of salvation." The helmet of salvation is another important piece of the armor of God. For a soldier, the helmet protects the brain. If a soldier gets hit in the head, without a helmet, it can be disorienting at the least and deadly at the worst. A soldier has been rendered helpless when they get a concussion. The helmet protects the head from concussions or death—without a helmet the head is exposed and vulnerable; with no helmet, a soldier feels vulnerable and apprehensive to get into a fight. Having no helmet exposes the soldier and they will fight much less aggressively or not fight at all. The helmet gives the soldier confidence to fight when he knows his head is protected.

Imagine if you were made to play in a football game but you were the only player not allowed to wear a helmet. How confident would you feel if your head is exposed? You wouldn't be trying to score a point on the other team—you would be more interested in protecting your vulnerable head. You would not play football—you would be using all your energy and time to protect your head. You have effectively been taken out of the game when you do not have a helmet. Having a helmet gives you confidence.

When I put on the helmet, in the armor of God, it is considered remembering my salvation. The word salvation means deliverance from harm. Salvation and deliverance can be used interchangeably—salvation means deliverance or rescue.

When I put on the helmet of salvation, I am remembering that I have been rescued from hell and I belong to God's family now. From the moment I first surrendered my life to Jesus Christ until the day I die and go to heaven, I am saved—I have been saved from going to hell. I never have to worry about whether I am saved because I surrendered to Jesus when I was a child. I believe in "once saved, always saved." In John 5:24, Jesus said: "I tell you the truth, those who listen to my message and believe in God who sent me have *eternal* life. They will *never* be condemned for their sins, but they have *already* passed from death into life."

The abuse of my past wants to condemn me—it lies to me and says that I am bad. The abuse wants to condemn me by saying I am unworthy of anything good.

The moment I first accepted Jesus Christ as my Lord and savior, I was saved. The battle for my soul ended that day—I became a child of God. In John 10:27-28 Jesus said, "My sheep listen to my voice; I know them, and they follow me. I give them eternal life, and they will never perish. No one can snatch them out of my hand."

I find comfort in remembering that I am going to heaven and I cannot screw that up. No matter what I believe about myself, I am going to heaven. Even when I go through periods where I am raging at God and I am denying him, I will not lose my ticket into heaven.

If I reject God and say I will not have any more to do with him, I am still going to heaven because Jesus promised me. There have been times when I raged at God and hated him because I felt abandoned and condemned by God; I have felt condemned by my circumstances, so I have held God responsible for everything that is wrong in my life. I have cursed God during these times—I have raged at God in times of despair. Even if I took my own life in a fit of despair, I am going to heaven—suicide cannot separate me from God.

Knowing that I cannot lose my salvation compels me forward. I am putting on the helmet of salvation when I remind myself that I cannot lose my salvation. I am able to find peace when I meditate on the security I have in Christ. I find comfort in knowing that no matter what happens in my life, not even death will win in the end. It doesn't matter how I feel or what I believe, God has me in his hands.

When I remember the helmet of salvation, it equips me to focus on the hope that God has laid out before me. The devil wants to convince me that I am hopeless and lost—I only have to put on the helmet of salvation to defeat the shame that threatens to try and destroy me.

Remembering the helmet of salvation reminds me that I have won. I am standing in the winner's circle; I have nothing to fear. I became a winner the first moment I accepted Jesus as my Lord and savior. I am a winner because I chose love; I chose Jesus Christ—I am a winner because God says I am a winner. My dad said I was a loser, but the God of the universe says I am a winner—that's good enough for me.

CHAPTER 40

SWORD OF THE SPIRIT

All of the armor of God that I have mentioned thus far is defensive—the belt, breastplate, shoes, shield, and helmet are all defensive pieces. The last piece of the armor of God is the sword—the sword is an offensive weapon. Ephesians 6:17 says, "...and the sword of the Spirit, which is the word of God."

For the soldier, he needs a way to fight back; the sword is an offensive weapon. The sword can kill the enemy. It does no good to only be on the defensive—it is good to defend, but the soldier needs a weapon to kill his enemy. If the soldier has no ability to fight back, then eventually they will tire and be overwhelmed.

The word of God is the sword of the spirit. Scripture is the sword. Hebrews 4:12 says, "For the word of God is alive and active. Sharper than any double-edged sword, it penetrates even to dividing soul and spirit, joints and marrow; It judges the thoughts and attitudes of the heart."

I have found it true that scriptures are the actual words of God. Scripture has had a way of planting itself inside of me—I find myself remembering what God has said in the Bible when I struggle with sin. Scripture is always there, reminding me of who I am.

Memorizing Scripture in the past has empowered me today. I find that when Scripture is hidden in my heart that it protects me from sin. I can use my own strength to battle temptation, but it is useless compared to using scripture to battle sin.

I find myself using a lot of words to rationalize why I shouldn't do something, but when a scripture comes to mind it brings closure to the discussion. Scripture has a way of getting straight to the point. I have found that Scripture *always* says it better than me—it is good for me to examine my thoughts and motives, but if I don't pass those thoughts through Scripture, then what I believe is incomplete.

In the beginning, shame was my foundation. I was told lies about who I am—I was a chaotic mess; I had no center; I was a shattered person.

When I began to see the Bible as an authority, God's word began to create a framework within me. God's word is reliable—God put me back together again with his words. Scripture introduced a new perspective. God's words built a foundation for me.

Reading God's word began my conversation with God; scripture brought me to life. God's word is not only words; they are life itself.

In Genesis, God spoke the world into existence. When God speaks, it is not words; it is a living, breathing conversation. When man speaks, we speak in our native language, trying to explain the world around us. There are many different languages and many different ways to try and explain what we experience in the world.

When God speaks it is different. God's word *is* truth. When God speaks, what he says is universal for every person in the world. Language is not a barrier when God speaks; language is only a barrier to us. God does not speak in signs and symbols like we do—when God speaks, he is truth.

For example, when I say house, I am speaking about a house. When God says, house, a literal house comes out of his mouth. God spoke the world into existence—God's words are life; God's words are power. John 1:1 says, "In the beginning was the Word, and the Word was with God, and the Word was God."

When I read Scripture, it has the authority of life itself. The Bible is God's word. God's words transformed me from a lifeless chaotic mass into a beautiful song. God's words moved through me and transformed me from a child of wrath into a child of the living God.

My existence is a miracle—God breathed his breath into me. Genesis 2:7 says, "Then the Lord God formed man from the dust of the ground and breathed the breath of life into his nostrils, and the man became a living being."

Scripture has moved into me and replaced the lies. God gave me the Bible so I could learn about him; God gave me the Bible so I could become free and find my proper place in the universe. 2 Timothy 3:16-17 says, "All scripture is God-breathed and is useful for teaching, rebuking, correcting, and training in righteousness, so that the servant of God may be thoroughly equipped for every good work."

Scripture is the actual words of God—the Bible is not a book about God; it is God communicating directly to me. When I read Scripture and pray, I am conversing with God—what a privilege!

CHAPTER 41

Pray at All Times

Prayer is simply talking to God; prayer is having a conversation and sharing the deepest desires of my heart with God. Ephesians 6:18 says, "Pray in the spirit at all times, with every kind of prayer and petition..." I find that I pray regularly to God out of the neediness of my heart.

I bring my doubts to the Lord—I don't hold back. Sometimes I am irreverent toward God in my prayer; I can yell at God and say I hate him and tell him he doesn't exist. After having a terrifying father, it was scary to talk to God the father. I would think, "If there is a God that exists, he must be terrible. I hate what he has done with this world." I found myself cursing God at times because I was exasperated from being in pain and afraid. I believe those were prayers to God.

In the beginning, I would yell at God and hate him. I would cry out in rage at the injustice I was experiencing; I would beg him to reveal himself to me. I felt justified in my rage because of all the horror I had experienced as an innocent child. It felt terrible to talk to God in this way, but it's the only faith I had at the time. I was terrified of God because I was afraid that he was the same as my biological father. I hated God but I would storm the gates of heaven with righteous indignation.

I demanded answers—I had no strength for any other prayer with God because I wanted an honest relationship with God. It was how I honestly felt. I demanded answers from God because he claimed to be good, yet I could not see good from where I was standing. I was apprehensive about talking to God this way, but I didn't know if he was even real. I could have been talking to the four walls of my house for all I knew.

I am bold in my conversations with God—I don't hold back. I am authentic in my prayers. I need God to be all good and all powerful; I need a strong God to lead me. I wasn't going to trust in anything that made me vulnerable to mean people. In the beginning, I wanted to believe in God, but God needed to be safe. I was scared out of my mind, and I was hoping that God wasn't anything like my father.

My prayers were desperate in the beginning—I had no reason to believe that love existed anywhere in the universe. I was abused by my father and abandoned by my mother, so my prayers expressed this reality.

I assumed that if God was good then he must be disgusted with me; I was unable to approach him without resentment. I hated God but I was also desperate for God. I felt humiliated by my desire to seek God. God let me be horribly abused and didn't do anything to help me. I had some serious questions that needed to be answered.

That is how I prayed to God in the beginning—these prayers were authentic; my prayers were an effort to reach out into the abyss and find something. My heart was damaged and empty; my heart was that of a wounded and helpless child. I was seeking help, while at the same time trying to protect myself from being hurt. I was courageously and boldly turning to God at the risk of finding out that there is no God. I was terrified that I would only find an empty abyss of meaninglessness. I was loving God in my attempts to turn to him. I didn't understand that I was loving God by seeking him until much later.

I was testing God. 1 John 4:1 says, "Beloved, do not believe every spirit, but test the spirits to see whether they are from God. For many false prophets have gone into the world." I was seeking what is good. I demanded excellence and God answered—God has not disappointed me.

This was my prayer life in the beginning—I see that God was pleased I was seeking him. I didn't want to believe that I could hurt this God I was seeking; if I can damage God, then he must be weak is what I believed. I was pouring my hurts into God. I came to realize that God can handle my outrage; God can handle my accusations. God is much bigger than anything I have experienced. My pain runs deep, but God runs deeper—that was my prayer life.

I was a violently abused child that had been abandoned by my parents. I came to realize that Jesus Christ is holy and perfectly good in every way. Jesus is love; Jesus is truth; Jesus is justice.

Jesus also suffered innocently at the hands of evil people. Jesus was humiliated, tortured, then killed horribly because he was all good. I found an advocate in Jesus when I found that he was not like my father. As an innocent victim, I have found Jesus to be my greatest advocate. Jesus knows what it is like to have your innocence torn from you violently and then to be abandoned; Jesus understands me. 1 John 4:4 says, "You, little children, are from God and have overcome them, because greater is he who is in you than he who is in the world."

My prayers with Jesus changed as I became convinced that he had nothing to do with my abuse. I came to understand that mankind is the problem, not God. My dad was cruel and my mother abandoned me, not Jesus Christ. I have an opportunity to refuse what is evil and join Jesus Christ. I was created and given the gift of free will—I have the choice to follow God. I didn't have to be like my parents and abandon what is good; I have the opportunity to love—pure love—in return. Free will is a gift, and I was going to use it to take a terrible revenge on evil. I am using my free will to bring love into the world.

Evil hurt me, not God. Evil tried to destroy Jesus the same as me. My enemy is evil, not good. I love what is good and hate was is evil. Evil has not been successful at tricking me into believing that God is my enemy—I chose Jesus Christ. I choose the solution. I won't let bitterness twist me into a person that only wants revenge. I can see that evil wants to destroy me.

Jesus rescued me from evil—Jesus is truly my savior. I owe Jesus my life.

Over the years, I have inventoried my relationships. I went through every relationship and separated what was my responsibility with what was their responsibility. I took responsibility and did the work that others were unwilling to do.

I was mixed up in the beginning and my prayers reflected that. I had an inferiority complex; I was convinced that I was cursed and so I approached God as if I was cursed. I was hopeless, so I would pray in despair.

In hindsight, I see that Jesus wept with me. Jesus was empathizing with me. Jesus was there from the beginning, cheering for me and giving me every opportunity to choose what is good. I have had the privilege of loving my creator in return. 1 John 4:19 says, "We love because he first loved us."

With my free will, I choose love because love has been there, all along, making my heart ache for what is good. God has been overwhelming me with love through my new family. My wife and my daughter are privileges—I get to experience their love as I lead the way in love. I am grateful to God that I get to love. I choose love, not bitterness—I choose Jesus Christ.

CHAPTER 42

HUMAN RIGHTS

I didn't believe I had human rights from the beginning. Because I was humiliated and abused, I did not believe I had the same human rights as others. I felt no sense of entitlement from being abused. Rights are an entitlement—I would have to believe myself to be inherently deserving of privileges or special treatment to exercise my rights. I felt cursed, debased, unclean, and condemned. I was unable to exercise my rights. I didn't believe I had rights. Human rights were something others enjoyed—I saw no avenue to be able to claim my rights.

I was hopelessly condemned—I had to be fixed; I had to be changed. This life was a loss; I had to be someone else to have rights. I had to be born again to have rights. I was broken beyond repair. Rights were for the privileged, not for subhuman garbage like me. I needed to be fixed—I needed to be made right. My only hope was to be reborn into another family. I was hopeless.

I was ready to receive Jesus Christ when he was introduced to me. I was in a state of condemnation and hopelessness; I was in a constant state of despair. I needed a miracle to change.

Jesus brought his extraordinary message through ordinary means—there was nothing particularly sensational happening at the time. I had been dragged to another church, and I was minding my own business when a stranger told me the answer to a puzzle that I could not solve. I was sitting condemned when Jesus spoke to me through a kind and gentle man. I was told about Jesus and what he did for me—Jesus used that man as a catalyst for his message of hope to me. Jesus told me that I needed to be reborn in him to be saved from condemnation. Jesus told me that he had the power to help me if I wanted his help. I knew I was hopeless, so I immediately said yes to Jesus.

The moment I surrendered to Jesus Christ I was made righteous—I was born again. I got a second chance. I was a lost child that was found by his true father. I was made right when I was reunited with my king and father, Jesus Christ. Jesus has shown me that I am entitled to receive my human rights. I have changed. I believe I have human rights today.

My Father turned out to be a king. I became a rags-to-riches story in that moment. I inherited the rights of my Father; I was made righteous in that moment. I had been made righteous so I could claim the human rights that were afforded me; I had been given the authority to stand up for myself. I was no longer a slave to my earthly birthright. My earthly birthright was fake—my home was with my father and king, Jesus Christ. I can exercise my rights as a full and legitimate human being. 2 Corinthians 5:17 says, "Therefore, if anyone is in Christ, the new creation has come: The old has gone, the new is here."

I began to fight back against the oppressions around me when I started to realize I had rights. I no longer accepted being treated poorly—Jesus gave me a voice to speak up for the abuses that happened to me. I could no longer tolerate being marginalized and ignored. For the first time in my life, my value was bigger than my fear. I could speak up in the face of punishment. My voice became more important than fear of suffering or death. My fear of having no voice replaced my fear of being tortured, humiliated, or even killed. Jesus Christ gave me what I needed to stand up for myself. 1 Peter 1:23 says, "For you have been born again, not of perishable seed, but of imperishable, through the living and enduring word of God." I became a new creation in Christ.

CHAPTER 43

I Have Peace

The world's definition of peace is to be free from all trouble. Peace is something to be attained. People talk about finding peace—peace is a pursuit, for most. Peace is sought after but remains elusive to those who seek it. The Oxford dictionary defines peace as "freedom from disturbance: tranquility."

I believe peace can only be found through Jesus Christ. According to the Bible a person can have peace amidst strife and war. Jesus said in John 16:33: "I have told you these things, so that in me you may have peace. In this world you will have trouble. But take heart! I have overcome the world." A person can have family, money, power, and success, yet have no peace—a person can achieve everything they ever wanted and not have peace; peace is not achieved or earned.

The Bible's definition of peace means "to be complete" or "to be sound." I was made complete the moment I accepted Jesus Christ as my Lord and savior. Sound means competent or reliable—my beliefs are sound. 2 Timothy 1:7 says, "I refuse to give into my fears. For God did not give me a spirit of fear, but of power and of love and of a *sound* mind." As I go through difficulty, I have found my belief in Jesus Christ has sustained me.

The apostle Paul said in Philippians 4:6-7: "Be anxious for nothing, but in everything, by prayer and petition, with thanksgiving, present your request to God. And the peace of God, which surpasses all understanding, will guard your hearts and minds in Christ Jesus." Finding peace is elusive to all who seek it. The peace of God is said to surpass all understanding. I have found peace to be a feeling that resonates deeply within me—that feeling says that everything is going to work out in the end, despite what I see happening today.

I find a quiet peace, like a still, small voice, underneath the turmoil in my life, sustaining me. Because I surrendered to God, I am no longer trying to bend the world to suit me. I am not trying to force the world to do what I want. I have stopped playing God; I have attained peace through surrender. I let God run the universe and I only take care of what is on my plate today.

I have found peace amid turmoil when I stop trying to control the outcomes in life. Peace is the confidence I have that God is ultimately responsible for taking care of me—I have peace because I know that death isn't the end; suffering isn't forever.

I have peace because I have seen God working in my life. I have seen God help me through sending me my wife to help me. My wife is a miracle in my life; I would not be where I am at today if she did not selflessly take care of me. My daughter is a manifestation of God's love. I have seen God come through for me time and time again. God has been bringing about miracles in my life—these miracles are real and able to be measured. I can look back at my life and see patterns of God's handiwork.

There are times where I have given up, but I found myself compelled to continue because of the undeniable comfort I find in the privileges of being in God's family. The privilege manifests itself when I find my identity in Jesus Christ. I identify with the universal and timeless themes of the ages. Jesus Christ is love—when

I identify with Jesus Christ, I am identifying with love. God created me—he gave me free will; I chose him and now I get to enjoy peace amid turmoil because I do not identify with the things of this world.

I can identify with the apostle Paul. Philippians 4:11-13 says, "I am not saying this because I am in need, for I have learned to be content whatever the circumstances. I know what it is to be in need, and I know what it is to have plenty. I have learned the secret of being content in any and every situation, whether well fed or hungry, whether living in plenty or in want. I can do all this through him who gives me strength." I also find a deep and strong contentment growing inside of me as I walk in relationship with Jesus Christ.

I do not identify with the world's definition of success. The world's success comes and goes like the tide at the beach. The world's success is unreliable and unpredictable—I do not trust in things that rust and things that moths can destroy. I do not trust in fleeting feelings that are here one minute and gone the next.

I identify with the universal and timeless theme of love. God is love; therefore, my life flows from love and what I do manifests love. My life has produced my marriage and my daughter because of my love for God. I did not have family values in the beginning, but those family values flowed out of my love for God. I was surprised to see my desires change from seeking self-gratification to seeking the things that sustain. God is changing me—love is changing me.

I have found, in my journey, that love is stronger than death and fear. Love is deeper than my deepest pain. Jesus Christ is the sacrifice I needed to be able to believe in love. In his sacrifice, I have learned that love conquers all. Philippians 4:8-9 says, "Finally, brothers, whatever is true, whatever is honorable, whatever is right, whatever is pure, whatever is lovely, whatever is admirable—if anything is excellent or praiseworthy—think on these things. Whatever you have learned or received or heard from me, or seen in me, put it into practice. And the God of Peace will be with you."

The good news is that God became man in the person Jesus Christ in order to reach me and tell me that I am loved. Jesus is the only person who has *always* been there for me and *never* let me down. Jesus rescued me from child abuse and set me up as a prince in his kingdom; I have been adopted into the royal family. Jesus loves a story of redemption, and I am a story of redemption.

www.ingramcontent.com/pod-product-compliance
Lightning Source LLC
LaVergne TN
LVHW041707060526
838201LV00043B/613